Super Prest

CW00749899

Hebble

Keith Healey & Nicholas Harris

Editor: John Banks

Cover: Stage carriage operations ended for Hebble on 28th February 1971 and No. **618** (**PCP 416**) collects passengers in Bradford's Chester Street bus station for the final route 7 journey to Halifax via Queensbury. The vehicle was one of a March 1962 batch of four AEC MD3RV Regents with Northern Counties 65-seat bodywork. It was sold to a dealer in April 1971. *(Peter Cain)*

Rear cover: Bus timetables are among the more ephemeral of printed publications. Designed for a season's use, they were expected to be thrown away at the end of their currency. Despite being economically produced with that short life in mind, they have survived in some numbers: a great boon to the transport researcher. There never was a period when their covers were works of art and perhaps the 1960s saw some of the blandest of them; Hebble's June 1965 offering was typical. *(John Banks Collection)*

Title page: All except four of Hebble's AEC Regents carried Roe bodywork. The exceptions were of type 9613A, which carried Willowbrook bodies. Number **268** (**CJX 69**) is seen turning into Chester Street bus station, Bradford, having travelled from Bingley on route 19. *(R F Mack)*

Opposite page: In 1951 [2] and 1952 [4] Hebble took delivery of six Leyland PSU1/15 Royal Tigers with Leyland 41-seat centre-entrance coach bodies. Number **26** (**CCP 224**) was the second in the batch and was withdrawn in 1964. It is seen in Bradford waiting to leave for Blackpool. *(D Akrigg)*

Below: This photograph was taken shortly after Halifax's Crossfield Road bus station opened in 1954 and shows three of Hebble's early postwar vehicles. In the bus station is No. **15** (**JX 9826**), one of the fifteen 1947 Roe-bodied AEC 0662 Regals and in Great Albion Street on the right is No. **1** (**GRR 311**), one of a pair of Weymann-bodied Leyland PS1 Tigers acquired in 1947 from East Midland Motor Services Ltd. Behind the ex-East Midland machine is one of a dozen 1946 AEC Regals with similar bodies. The splendid building - the Alhambra - in the background was shortly to be demolished and the land used as a bus park. *(D Akrigg Collection/J Copland)*

Editor's note and acknowledgements

If the rules of logic were to apply Hebble Motor Services should not have existed after it became a BET subsidiary in 1932. Its area of operation was only 28 miles east to west and 24 miles north to south and in fact it was less because no routes went beyond Bingley although their boundary extended as far as Skipton. It had three Joint Omnibus Committees in its area plus various municipalities and was surrounded by five large companies. It became one of two companies owned by British Electric Traction as against the Tilling and British Automobile Traction Company that had no private shareholders, all shares being divided between BET and the railways, each with a 50% holding; the other was Hebble's neighbour Yorkshire (Woollen District) Transport. The registered office of Hebble for most of its life was at 88 Kingsway in London and, as will be seen, it survived for another forty years.

Hebble's history is closely involved with its three nearest municipal neighbours: Halifax, Bradford and Huddersfield; sometimes more detail than may seem necessary is given to them, but it all relates to the unusual circumstances under which Hebble had to operate.

The text of this survey of Hebble was written by Keith Healey; information for captions was prepared by Nicholas Harris; picture research and selection has been the series editor's province. Don Akrigg has generously made his comprehensive Hebble photographic collection available, without which the illustrative content would have been much the poorer; all illustrations are individually acknowledged in the captions.

One cannot write about Hebble without referring to Norman Dean, who from 1922 to 1939 was the principal figure behind the development of the company, and his paper *"My first seventeen years in management"*, presented to The Omnibus Society in 1959, has been a valuable source of information for the 1920s.

John Senior has read and annotated the proofs, as has Ron Maybray; John D Watson has been of much help; and David and Mary Shaw have acted as proof readers - many thanks to all.

As always with volumes in this series, no claim is made that this work is a definitive history complete in every detail: rather is it an illustrated overview of Hebble's vehicles and services throughout its existence. For a complete history of the fleet the reader is recommended to the new publication on the Company from our friends of The PSV Circle.

John Banks
Romiley, Cheshire
January 2004

The Story of Hebble

The beginning 1924 - 1929

The brothers Oliver and Charles Holdsworth in 1918 were haulage contractors in Halifax with an excursion business as a sideline. They had also acquired in the same year a taxi and funeral business.

In 1922 the brothers were persuaded to commence a bus service between Harrogate and Bilton to operate every ten minutes on a circular route. After three months they were hit by a disastrous fire which destroyed the four vehicles based at Mornington Crescent, Harrogate. Further vehicles were obtained including a rebuild of one caught in the fire and the services recommenced operating until February 1924 when the Bilton Motor Company, as it was now called, was purchased by the Harrogate Road Car Company, which a month later was in turn to be subject to a takeover - jointly by the British Automobile Traction Company and Thomas Tilling.

This brought Norman Dean, who was the Holdsworth's nephew, back to Halifax from Harrogate where he had been managing the business on their behalf. He suggested operating in the Halifax area and on 1st December 1924 two routes commenced: one between Halifax and Brighouse and the other between Halifax and Bingley. Licences were obtained from these two towns as well as others en route but Halifax refused to licence the services. The Holdsworths

The Hebble fleet was an Albion stronghold for many years: the first were delivered in 1926 and the last in 1940. Number **105 (JX 1402)** was one of a batch of six of type PW67 with Brush bodywork. New in 1934, it was requisitioned by the Ministry of Transport in 1940, returned in 1946 and scrapped. It is illustrated in Alexandra Street, Halifax, on a route 28 timing to Rochdale. This service had been taken over from the railways in December 1933. *(John Banks Collection)*

purchased a plot of land in Commercial Street, Halifax to use as a terminus. They were well aware of the problems operating from Halifax without licences and they did not allow any passenger joining at Halifax to alight until the end of the tram route, in the case of the Bingley service, or the end of the borough boundary on the Brighouse service, approximately 1½ miles from the town centre in both cases. However, the police decided to take action against the Holdsworths for picking up and setting down the same passenger within the borough, although this was later changed to picking up within the borough without a licence. There was at that time much controversy taking place about the role of councils being responsible for the issue of licences to operate services, when some councils had the vested interest of owning and operating transport services within their borough.

To try and overcome the problems of not being licensed, the Holdsworths decided that only passengers who had booked their ticket in advance at the ticket office on private land would be picked up within the borough. Again the police stepped in, resulting in fines by the local magistrates; the next idea was to pick up only holders of return tickets, i.e. those booked from outside the borough from areas where licences were held. The police then resorted to the use of plain-clothes officers who attempted to board vehicles without having a return ticket.

In the meantime two further services were commenced, in 1925, this time from Halifax to Elland and also to Greetland but still operating on the return ticket principle in Halifax. The Greetland service was soon extended to Barkisland and the Elland service continued into Huddersfield: the latter also refused to grant licences so again the return ticket system had to be used, in this case from both termini.

Shortly after the commencement of this service the North Western Road Car Company started a service from Oldham to Elland. They were also refused a licence to extend to Halifax and they approached the Holdsworths to see if arrangements could be made to operate from Elland to Halifax on the return ticket basis. North Western also wished to reach Huddersfield and, although involving a roundabout route, Elland looked a possible connecting point. Various discussions took place

between the two operators but nothing could be resolved.

The whole position on the system of operations as far as the Holdsworths were concerned was very unsatisfactory and, with the backing of hundreds of passengers, appeals were lodged with the Ministry of Transport against the refusal of Halifax and Huddersfield to grant licences. The Inspector appointed by the Minister heard the appeals in Halifax and some months later the Minister instructed that licences should be granted to the Holdsworths but with protective fares over the tram routes, which, rather ironically, was what the Holdsworths had originally wanted to do.

Some routes were refused by the Minister, mainly to Ripponden which were covered by other operators. The Halifax - Huddersfield via Elland route was to become a joint operation with Holdsworth having 50% and Halifax and Huddersfield 25% each.

By now the bus side of the Holdsworth business was becoming known as "Hebble" rather than Holdsworth. They never formed a company under that name but buses always carried the name "The Hebble" or "Hebble", after a local brook. From this point it will be referred to as Hebble in the text.

The grant of licences by Halifax enabled Hebble to get away from the private ground and pick up in the street with Alexandra Street and King Edward Street being used by their services. All this had happened by October 1925.

Application was then made for two other routes from Halifax, one to Luddenden and the other to Beech Road, Sowerby Bridge. Again Halifax refused licences and the services were operated on the return ticket basis using the Commercial Street site.

The 1926 General Strike gave Hebble the chance to introduce new services as they, like most small operators, had no agreements with any trade unions. Three routes were operated to Bradford, Leeds and Manchester. At the end of the strike the first two routes continued but that to Manchester was withdrawn. Bradford granted licences but again Halifax refused, later changing their mind. Leeds, after consideration, refused a licence as did Halifax on that route and again the service was operated on the return ticket basis from each terminus. There was an

Most bus companies' crews have troubles in winter driving conditions but perhaps Hebble's had more than most in the rugged districts they served. Nevertheless, the Company had a reputation for maintaining services no matter how bad the conditions. **CP 7578** was an Albion PMA28 new in 1929 with a Ramsden fully fronted coach body as fleet number 75. It was rebodied by Eastern Counties in 1935 with the bus body shown above and renumbered as **120** *(see also page 23)*. It was withdrawn in 1946. Number **45** (**BJX 56**) was a type 9612E AEC Regent III with Roe lowbridge bodywork, one of three new in 1950. In this shiver-inducing scene it is seen in Queensbury bound for Halifax on route 17. *(Hebble Collection)*

alternative service operated by Yorkshire (WD) but this was routed via Cleckheaton. A further route was opened in late 1926 from Queensbury via Thornton and Allerton to Bingley. January 1927 saw a service between Brighouse and Bradford which gave protection to the Bradford tram route that operated over part of the route.

It was only a matter of time before competition came in the form of the Calder Bus Company of Bailiff Bridge, near Brighouse. Two of their services from Brighouse to Bradford competed with Hebble. In 1927 a new Hebble service between Halifax and Heptonstall began, quickly followed by Halifax - Hebden Bridge and Blackshaw Head, both having to operate on the return ticket basis in Halifax.

By this time the size of the fleet had increased so much that it brought problems to the Holdsworth haulage depot in Darley Street and their funeral department at Gibbet Hill; both places had been pressed into service to deal with the maintenance of the bus fleet and many vehicles had to be parked on open ground overnight in Commercial Street. A building, previously used as a dye works by a subsidiary of the Bradford Dyers Association, in Walnut Street, Halifax was purchased and brought into use as a bus garage in August 1927.

In the same month the Blackshaw route was extended into Burnley who granted a licence after protection was given to their local bus route which covered approximately 2½ miles of the route out of Burnley to Mereclough.

By now Hebble were concentrating on the Albion chassis for their fleet and in the first instance bodies were built by local firms and, according to Garcke's Guide of 1928, O & C Holdsworth owned 88 vehicles comprising 12 Leyland 4-ton wagons, 6 Leyland and Albion motor coaches (18-, 26- or 28-seaters), 12 Leyland omnibuses, 45 Albion omnibuses, 6 Karrier omnibuses and 7 Rolls-Royce hire cars.

The influx of operators into Halifax, although on the return ticket basis, affected the Corporation's revenue and new services were put into operation by them. Operation outside the municipal boundary was also considered to such places as Oldham, Rochdale, Keighley and Leeds. The first route was to Rochdale which commenced on 28th August 1926.

In 1927 Oldham Corporation was also seeking powers to operate outside their boundary, one of the proposed routes being between Halifax and Oldham via Sowerby Bridge and Ripponden. The North Western Road Car Company objected to these proposals and, just before the hearing, agreement was reached for the company to participate in the service which commenced on Friday 15th April, 1927. At the same time the North Western route from Oldham to Elland was extended into Halifax although this was withdrawn in October.

There were problems with the West Riding County Council who seemed to find as many objections as possible to municipalities operating long-distance services over their roads. Their principal objection was that the vehicles were not suitable and caused damage to the roads. They stopped Oldham and Halifax operating between those two towns, which left North Western as the sole operator. It also opposed the Halifax - Rochdale route which was jointly operated by these two Corporations. North Western was approached by Rochdale to operate the route but Halifax would not agree to this arrangement and on 1st December 1928 the London Midland & Scottish Railway took over the route using their railway stations as terminal points, which made the route mileage longer than necessary. By this time talks were taking place between Halifax and the railways regarding an area scheme, hence Halifax's reluctance to involve North Western.

Nineteen-twenty-eight saw further extensions to Hebble's operations, starting with the purchase of Hugh Brigg and Sons, who operated around the Bingley area. There were originally two related Briggs operating in the area but Hugh Brigg purchased the business of his relative. It was arranged after the takeover that the vehicles to operate these services would be garaged at Messrs J W North Ltd in Legrams Lane, Bradford, in which the Holdsworths had a financial interest, to avoid the dead mileage from Halifax. A new service between Halifax and Bradford was commenced via Queensbury and this, together with the service via Shelf, gave a combined frequency of ten minutes during most of the day.

In common with others, Bradford Corporation was looking at ways of operating bus services outside the municipal boundary and in October 1928 had a Bill going through

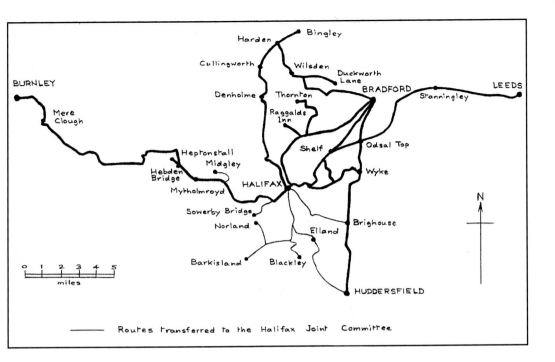

Above: Hebble services in 1929 including details of those routes transferred to the Halifax Joint Omnibus Committee in November of that year. *(Map drawn for this book)*

Below: Hebble bus routes and express services as operating in the summer of 1955. Taken together, these activities covered the modest north-south distance of Bingley to Rochdale and, more ambitiously, from the west coast at Blackpool to its counterpart on the east, Scarborough. *(John Banks Collection)*

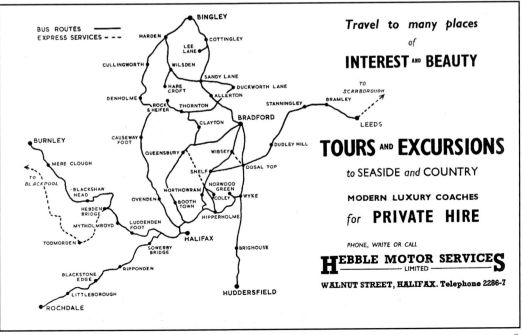

Parliament. The small village of Bailiff Bridge, which was the operating area of the Calder Bus Company, was the key point in the Bill. On the same day as the Bill was to be heard Bradford signed an agreement with Calder to purchase the business for £22,500 including vehicles: a simple transaction but, as one trade paper put it, "a most curious situation arose". Although Bradford had gained running powers to Halifax and Huddersfield, neither of the two towns would licence their vehicles; in fact Halifax refused Bradford permission to run buses over their tram track between Brighouse and Bailiff Bridge.

Brighouse Council, who were the licensing authority, called a meeting of the three Councils to try and resolve the situation. The Bradford representatives left the meeting early as no mutually satisfactory arrangement was possible for continuing the Calder services.

Bradford then came to an agreement with Hebble for them to operate the ex-Calder route between Halifax and Wyke and part of another Calder route between Hipperholme and Bradford on a fixed rate per mile. Hebble also participated in a 20-minute service between Bradford and Brighouse on the proportion of Huddersfield two and Hebble one vehicle until such time as Bradford were ready and willing to operate on the service.

Bradford and Halifax then reached agreement whereby Bradford would pay Halifax £7,500 and out of that sum Halifax would pay for the Brighouse - Bailiff Bridge road to be repaired after the removal of the tram tracks; Halifax would also cease to run along that road with any type of vehicle thus enabling Bradford to operate a service to Brighouse and later into Huddersfield. The service commenced on 31st March 1929.

On 29th April at a meeting of the Bradford Tramways Committee the Chairman stated that it had not been possible to take the committee or even the council fully into confidence on the Calder Bus Company purchase as negotiations had been of such a delicate character and were even at that moment not fully settled. Confirmation was given that the Calder fleet had been sold for £5,000: although it was not specified that it had gone to Hebble; the two routes operated on behalf of Bradford were also transferred to Hebble.

Meanwhile, on 15th May 1929, North Western had extended their Halifax - Oldham route into Manchester and in July the route was extended to commence from Bradford, with Yorkshire (WD) being later involved in the operation. Short-distance fares were available and the service operated every two hours.

Ripponden & District who also operated between Halifax and Manchester then extended their route to commence at Bradford but because of licence refusal they operated on the return ticket basis.

Railway Involvement and Agreements 1928 - 1932

Prior to the amalgamation of the various railway companies into the Big Four - the London Midland & Scottish, the London & North Eastern, the Great Western and the Southern - some of the constituent companies had had powers to operate road services; the old Great Western took most advantage of these powers, but some of the others were not far behind. In order to put the position on a proper footing each of the aforementioned railways presented a Bill to Parliament in 1928 for consent to operate road passenger transport services.

The pros and cons of the Bills were submitted to a Joint Select Committee of the Lords and Commons to consider the proposals. Among the railway evidence was that local bus services were eroding into their receipts and the Sheffield area was quoted as an example: with 200 miles of line and 24 stations the railway's takings had gone down by 29.56% in three years on local services; all the railways wanted to was to participate on the same basis as the other operators to protect their business - what in today's jargon would be referred to as a "level playing field".

Included in the Bill was a clause that the railway bus services would not operate in the London Metropolitan Area and in the Provinces protection would be given to services operated by the municipalities within their boundaries. A further amendment to extend the protection outside the boundary on services operated by local authorities, which was proposed by Sheffield and supported by others, was defeated.

The Bill was passed in August 1928 giving the railways several options: to begin services

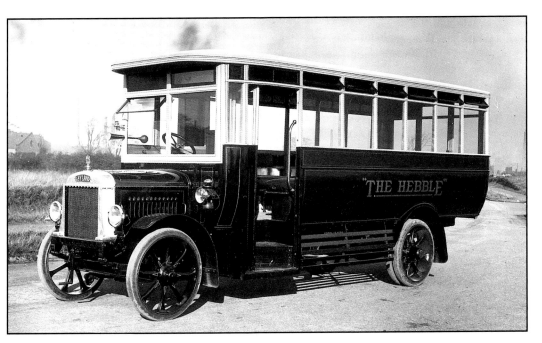

Above: Number **2** (**CP 3736**) was a Leyland A13 with a 26-seat Stockton-style body, also by Leyland. New in November 1924, it was withdrawn in 1928 and saw further service with Burnley Corporation Tramways and its successors until April 1936. The fleetname "The Hebble", used only on the first four vehicles, was soon replaced by "Hebble", as seen below.

Below: Number **5** (**CP 3804**) was a Leyland SG9 with Leyland 38-seat bodywork. In later life the vehicle was converted for use as a removal van for a London firm and was licensed as such until April 1952. All but part of the cab was subsequently destroyed by fire but some parts of the remaining vehicle were used in the restoration of a 1923 Leyland SG7 DM 2583. The registration number survives on a private car. *(Both: John Banks Collection)*

in their own right; to purchase companies and operate them: or, as it was within their powers, to supply financial aid and purchase shares in bus companies, but not control them. Their first move was to approach various municipalities in Lancashire and Yorkshire to operate and adopt area schemes. The Lancashire municipalities were not interested but Halifax, Huddersfield, Sheffield and Todmorden were and area operating agreements were arranged. These were based on a simple area formula. All services operated within the borough boundary would be operated by the Corporation who would keep all the receipts.

The next area, in the case of Halifax, was referred to by their officers as the Red Area, mainly because it was outlined in red on the map, and this extended to a radius of approximately ten miles from the town centre. All services operated by the Corporation into the Red Area would be operated by the Joint Omnibus Committee. Services operated from these two areas to places outside the Red Area would be operated by the railways or their nominee. The JOC would have a separate fleet with the vehicles to be owned jointly by Halifax and the railway although the livery was the distinctive Halifax colours. Passengers would be able to travel on any vehicle in any area with the revenue received being appropriated accordingly.

The railways were now looking for a company to operate the services outside the Halifax agreed area; they had not yet come to an agreement with the newly formed Tilling/BAT Company over joint shareholding. Had it been otherwise this story would no doubt have been very different. The largest concern in Halifax was Hebble and the Holdsworth brothers were approached by the railways to see if they were willing to sell. Agreement was reached and signed on 30th April 1929, to take effect from 1st January of the same year. The Holdsworths were to manage the concern on behalf of the railways at no charge until 31st December.

It is reported that the railways paid £165,000 for the Hebble business and this amount included the purchase of the Calder vehicles from Bradford. It is open to conjecture if Hebble was worth that much. W J Crosland Taylor made the comment when Crosville was railway-owned that railway money was plentiful and the operators the railway had purchased to merge later into Crosville were obtained at prices out of all proportion to their value. By mid 1930 the railways had spent £7.5 million investing in road passenger companies.

Meanwhile the railways had reached agreement with Halifax and on 1st April 1929 the Joint Omnibus Committee came into being with the railways purchasing vehicles from the Corporation to operate their part of the services.

A further agreement was signed between the railways and Halifax whereby the Corporation would purchase the former Holdsworth 50% interest in the Huddersfield service (operated jointly with Halifax and Huddersfield, who each had a 25% interest) and a half interest in the Hebble routes operated wholly within the specified area, this to include vehicles.

The services to be transferred were:

Halifax - Barkisland and Norland via Greetland
Halifax - Brighouse via Southowram
Halifax - Huddersfield via Elland
Halifax - Midgley via Luddenfoot
Halifax - Beech Road
Halifax - Hullen Edge via West Vale
Halifax - Heptonstall

The Halifax - Huddersfield route was outside the Red Area as far as Hebble were concerned, but because of the involvement of Huddersfield it was considered to be a Red Area service, with the boundary of this area from Halifax reaching the corresponding Huddersfield boundary.

Halifax JOC paid £36,000 for the seven routes and 13 vehicles and it would seem that 6th November 1929 was when the services and vehicles were transferred.

The newly formed Omnibus Society carried reports in their magazine of ex-Hebble vehicles operating on Halifax JOC routes in their old colours, which were described as being similar to the Great Western Railway's chocolate and cream livery, but with the fleetname painted out. In addition, some LMS buses were running on the Stainland, Heptonstall, Sowerby Bridge and Rishworth routes. Fleet number 18F (CH 7909), a Leyland Lion, for example, had the LMS coat of arms replaced by the Halifax JOC blue and red circle.

Above: Number **15** (**CP 4899**) was an Albion PK26 with a 26-seat body built by Fielding and Bottomley of Halifax. It was new in September 1926 and was sold in April 1932 to a Leeds operator who ran it until September 1937.

Below: Hebble bought only three new Karriers. That illustrated is No. **32** (**CP 6096**), a CL6 model with bodywork by Davidson. New to the fleet in September 1927, it passed to the Halifax Joint Omnibus Committee in November 1929. It was last licensed in December 1931 to a Welsh operator. *(Both: Hebble Collection)*

From 1st January 1930 the railways took over the control of Hebble from the Holdsworths, placing Norman Dean in charge; three Leyland Tigers with all weather bodies were transferred from the railways. Dean considered them superior to anything owned by the other Halifax operators and he used them to increase Hebble's private hire business.

Holdsworths had operated excursions to Blackpool since the early twenties with the route expanding into a daily service throughout the year. Ribble Motor Services were concerned that Hebble might ply for hire in the area west of Burnley and after an exchange of letters Burnley was to be considered as a border town between the two operators' areas.

In 1931 both Hebble and Yorkshire (WD) made similar applications to the newly formed Traffic Commissioners who were responsible for the issue of Road Service Licences instead of, as in the past, the local councils. This was for a service between Halifax and Manchester via Hebden Bridge, Todmorden, Littleborough, Rochdale and Middleton. The application was later withdrawn as no doubt Ribble as well as Rochdale and Todmorden objected to the proposal.

By now, discussions were taking place between the British Electric Traction Company and the railways over the future of the Hebble concern, and on 19th July 1930 the name Hebble Motor Services Ltd was registered at their address by the BET. The directors were D E Bell (General Manager of Yorkshire WD), F J Chappell (General Manager of West Yorkshire Road Car) and P M Rossdale (a BET Director), plus the three Railway nominees. This was to be a company owned jointly by Yorkshire Woollen District, West Yorkshire and the railways to operate the ex-Holdsworth routes. This did not occur because of, it is understood, the withdrawal of West Yorkshire from the scheme. Thus the routes remained under Railway control until 1932.

February 1932 was a busy time for signing agreements by the various officers of both the railways and BET. The first, on 22nd February, was for the sale by the railways of the former Holdsworth business to the newly formed Hebble Motor Services with its registered Office at 88 Kingsway in the County of London and having a nominal capital of 150,000 £1 shares.

The make-up of the Board had now changed: BET Directors had replaced Bell and Chappell, and the Board included such prominent BET men as Leo M Myers, J S Wills and W S Wreathall. The purchase price was £138,783/18/6d, of which three-quarters was to be paid to the LMSR and the other quarter to the LNER; the agreement was to come into force as and from 1st May 1930. As soon as possible after the completion of the agreement the BET were to subscribe and take up for cash 50,000 £1 shares with the LMSR taking up 37,500 and the LNER 12,500. A further £50,000 split between BET £25,000, LMSR £18,750 and LNER £6,250 was to be loaned to the company at the rate of 6% per annum repayable at the option of the company at any time. The railways were also to receive a profit payment amounting to £8,766/2/2d for the period 1st May 1930 to the selling date.

Included was the freehold plot of land on Walnut Street and all garages, offices, workshops and other buildings erected thereon. Also all the office and land in Commercial Street (exclusive of pumps, tanks and cigarette machines and one office). Seventy vehicles mainly Albion and Leyland but including a Dennis and a Commer which had been taken over with the Brigg services, were included. They were all single-deckers with the exception of four Leyland Titans. There was also a Karrier goods vehicle, fleet number 72.

The following routes as operated in May 1930 which had been licensed by the Traffic Commissioners were transferred:

Halifax - Bradford via Shelf
Halifax - Bradford via Queensbury
Halifax - Bingley
Halifax - Burnley
Bradford - Huddersfield
Halifax - Leeds
Bradford - Blackpool
Raggalds - School Green
Bradford - Bingley
Halifax - Wyke
Duckworth Lane - Bingley
Duckworth Lane - Wilsden
Hipperholme - Bradford

On the following day, 23rd February, a further agreement was signed between the

Above: Number **26** (**CP 5876**) was an Albion PM28 new in August 1927. It was photographed at Hebble's combined bus station, booking office and petrol station in Commercial Street, Halifax. A cinema was subsequently built on this site. The bus was sold in November 1932. *(Hebble Collection)*

Below: Massey-bodied Albion PK26 No. **14** (**CP 4897**) was new to Hebble in July 1926 and was sold in April 1932. *(Senior Transport Archive)*

railway companies and Hebble; this was known as a working agreement to define amongst other things the operating area of the company and naming the services which were not included in the agreement but had already been transferred to the Joint Omnibus Committee. The Halifax - Rochdale LMS service was also included. This agreement was for twenty years, backdated to 28th December 1929, which brought it into line with all the other agreements the railways had made with other T/BAT and BET companies.

One last agreement was signed on 24th February, this time between BET and the railways that in the event of any new share issue by Hebble, the first option must be given to the three companies on an equal basis.

Under BET Control 1932 - 1945

The new Company gave up the Bradford garage rented from J W North and transferred to the former West Yorkshire garage that had been obtained with the Blythe & Berwick business. Situated in Edderthorpe Street, it was shared with Yorkshire (WD). At the same time Hebble applied for the Scarborough licence issued to Yorkshire (WD). The service had been operated by Hebble vehicles "On Hire". This service, apart from that to Blackpool, was the only express service operated by Hebble for a good many years.

It would seem that bus companies could not operate without agreements and 1933 saw some more. On 20th February agreement was reached between Hebble and the railways whereby the Company was to pay the railways 35% of receipts for passengers picked up and set down in certain sections on certain routes within the Halifax operating area. It also included the proviso that if in the future the Rochdale - Halifax route was transferred by the railways to the Company then the 35% of receipts in a given section should also apply on this service.

Another agreement was on 5th October between Hebble and Rochdale whereby the Company would pay to the Corporation 10% of gross receipts from all passengers both picked up and set down in any one journey between Rochdale and Littleborough. This agreement was to come into force as and when Hebble took the service over from the LMSR, i.e. 10th December 1933.

The last 1933 agreement, on 13th December, was between the LMSR and Hebble, whereby the Halifax - Rochdale service was sold to Hebble for £1,500 and the Railway would not oppose the application to take the service away from railway stations. It also stated there was nothing in the agreement stopping the route being extended through to Manchester at one end or to Leeds or Bradford at the other end. The service would also be operated jointly with the North Western Road Car Company. North Western did apply for licences to operate but withdrew later as it could not agree to paying Rochdale 10% of gross receipts between Rochdale and Littleborough; this removed the likelihood of the service ever being extended into Manchester. There was a final clause that the four drivers and conductors employed by the railways should be offered employment. No vehicles were taken over, as they were retained by the LMSR. At last Hebble were able to serve Ripponden, a town they had tried to reach over the years.

The reasoning behind the remarks in the Editor's preamble, that after the purchase of the Holdsworth business from the railways it ought not to have survived, now comes to light. The involvement of the North Western Road Car Company was not a coincidence. The area agreement signed by that Company with the railways in 1929 shows their boundary running from Rochdale through Littleborough then Ripponden to Halifax; in fact such places as Sowerby Bridge, Greetland and Elland were within the North Western operating area, as their boundary then ran from Halifax down to Huddersfield via Fixby Hall then to Sheffield. The eastern side of the boundary was the operating areas of Yorkshire (WD) and Yorkshire Traction and Bradford was West Yorkshire and the road from Rochdale to Skipton was in the territory of Ribble.

In 1931 North Western and Yorkshire (WD) made further alterations by changing their boundaries to the part between Halifax and Huddersfield. The portion between Halifax and Elland became a joint road with either party at liberty to operate, and the road between Elland and Huddersfield moved into the territory of Yorkshire (WD).

When the Hebble working agreement was signed, its area of operation was overlaid on

Above: United Automobile Services Ltd, of Lowestoft, built the 26-seat coach body on Hebble's No. **45** (**UR 3763**), a Leyland Tiger TS2 that had been new in July 1929 to the London, Midland and Scottish Railway. It was transferred into the railway-owned Hebble fleet in 1930. The vehicle was fitted with a new Duple coach body in March 1937 and was renumbered 138. The chassis was scrapped in January 1947 and the body fitted to a new chassis (JX 9735). *(Hebble Collection)*

Below: In May 1929 Hebble purchased four Leyland TD1 Titans fitted with Leyland 51-seat bodies. The last of them was No. **69** (**CP 7576**), seen here when brand new. All four were withdrawn in October 1957. *(John Banks Collection)*

those of existing companies, who accepted the position so that Hebble could survive even though operating services into their areas; it was significant that no objection was raised but at the same time no concessions were given either. Therefore it was not surprising that the Yorkshire (WD) part of the Bradford - Manchester route was not transferred to Hebble.

In another example, Hebble had lost the service to Elland after the formation of the Joint Omnibus Committee, but there was still a service operated by E J Slater & Son which was purchased by Yorkshire (WD) in 1934. Slater operated two routes: Halifax - Sowerby Bridge and Halifax - Rastrick. A complicated financial arrangement was made between the JOC and Yorkshire (WD) whereby Yorkshire (WD) would cease to operate between Halifax and Elland but still operate from Elland to Lower Edge and Rastrick and the JOC would pass to Yorkshire (WD) their route between Brighouse and Lower Edge. In fact all these services were within the Hebble area, to whom they should have been passed.

Nineteen-thirty-four also saw the purchase of the Halifax excursion operator Robert Edwards and Company Ltd by Hebble with four vehicles taken over. The acquired company was operated as a subsidiary until being wound up on 30th May 1940 when the business was absorbed into the parent company.

In the same year, 1934, a Saturday only Halifax - Bradford service via Shelf and Wibsey was introduced. The route was approximately ½mile shorter than the other two routes enabling the return journey to be done in one hour. It earned the nickname "Wibsey Flyer" among the crews.

The Blackpool service was to be combined into the proposed Yorkshire - Blackpool Pool to be operated by West Yorkshire, Yorkshire (WD), Yorkshire Traction, Ribble Motor Services and Hebble; the latter had a 9% mileage and revenue entitlement in it. The actual Pool came into operation on 1st November, 1935 but was back dated to 1st December, 1934 for financial reasons.

Hebble received an ex-Walker Taylor Leyland TS2 coach as their part of the Pool's purchase of three Blackpool operators. Hebble also held shares in the newly built Coliseum coach station at Blackpool, which was owned by Blackpool Omnibus Stations Ltd. (The full story of this and other Yorkshire Coaching Pools in which Hebble were involved are detailed in the Prestige Series No. 22.)

In August 1935 the three routes Leeds - Halifax, Rochdale - Halifax and Burnley - Halifax were combined to operate with through running, thus avoiding the change at Halifax. In later years the Leeds - Halifax section of the Burnley route was normally worked by double-deckers, involving through passengers in a change at Halifax, although through ticketing continued.

In March 1936 Huddersfield Corporation were promoting a Bill in Parliament to add further powers with regard to their trolleybus operations for a route between Huddersfield and Bradley Bar. Agreement was reached where, if the route was granted, the adult single fare should not be more than ½d less than the fare charged by Hebble over the same route unless prior arrangement had been reached with the Company.

Nineteen-thirty-seven saw an unusual objection being lodged by Hebble and other operators against Halifax Corporation seeking permission to build a bus station in the town and it would be some years, 1954 in fact, before Halifax got its bus station. Even then Hebble, North Western and Yorkshire (WD) objected to their services being forced to use the station, known as Cross Field, and it was only after negotiations that they agreed.

Reference has been made to the 35% of net revenue paid to the railways over certain stages in the Halifax area. In 1938 this was reduced to 25% and during the 1960s it was changed to a set monthly figure, later becoming a quarterly payment.

In May 1939 Norman Dean left the Company to take up a similar position with Yorkshire Traction at Barnsley, so ending his seventeen years at Hebble, which had seen three different owners and in the last six years an increase of over 50% in passengers carried with a 24% increase in mileage. His place was taken by C R H Wreathall, who had been at Yorkshire Traction as Assistant to the General Manager.

However, things were about to change with the outbreak of the Second World War on 3rd September 1939. The war brought many problems to Hebble, as it did to other operators.

Number **68** (**CP 7575**), one of the four 1929 Leyland Titans, was sold in October 1937 and subsequently converted for use as a mobile first aid post in the County Borough of Southport. The ingenious "flat-pack" constructions on either side allowed the vehicle to carry two extra rooms around with it. *(Both: John Banks Collection)*

Services were cut, some withdrawn and restrictions were imposed by the Regional Transport Commissioners who had replaced the Traffic Commissioners. All services were operated under permits and fuel was rationed based on the mileage authorised by the RTC. Road staff joined the forces in droves and women were recruited as conductresses; some became drivers but there is no record of any at Hebble. Many employees would, after their turn of duty, go to their "second job" as members of the Home Guard, ARP Wardens, Auxiliary Fire Service or Special Constables. Even the Registered Office was moved from London to the Omnibus Station in Midland Street, Barnsley, together with some staff because of air raids on the Capital.

To cover extra services provided for workers there had to be an increase in the fleet, which, according to the yearly statistics supplied by the Company to the BET Board, stood at 62 vehicles on 31st March 1941 but by 31st March 1943 had risen to 81. There seems to be a mystery regarding the extra vehicles. It is believed that Hebble coordinated the works services operating to the A V Roe factory at Yeadon and to cover this hired in various vehicles, which were added to the fleet strength. Fuel was granted to the holder of the Road Service Permit not to the person owning the vehicle if they were different. Thus if Hebble had the permit to operate they could hire in vehicles up to the amount of mileage and fuel they were allowed by the RTC.

Although receipts increased, profits remained the same because the Government imposed EPT (Excessive Profit Tax) on companies who, through no fault of their own, had increased their profit over and above that which they would normally be expected to make. In 1941 the Company paid £14,200 in tax and by 1944 this had increased to £30,000 while retainable profit was around the £19,000 mark throughout the period.

In 1942 Tilling & BAT went into voluntary liquidation with the shares in the companies they controlled being passed to either the newly formed BET Omnibus Services owned by BET or to Thomas Tilling. This did not affect Hebble which was a direct BET Company.

Nineteen-forty-four saw the delivery of four Guy Arab utility-type double-deckers.

According to the returns on 31st March 1945, the fleet stood at 87 vehicles. Towards the end of June 1945 there was a relaxation in private hire and excursion operations. In the case of private hire the total mileage of 70 from garage back to garage was allowed and excursions were not allowed to exceed 50 miles.

The early postwar period 1946 - 1959

The resumption of express services brought about an increase in fares caused by extra costs, which had built up over the years. A general increase of 16⅔% was granted on all express routes but the day return fare between Yorkshire and Blackpool was increased by 25%. This also brought about requests from the trade unions for an increase in wages. BET were also looking at the salary of their General Managers. In the case of Hebble their present General Manager, R J White, received £700 p.a. plus a £100 war bonus and it was proposed the maximum salary be increased to £1,000. This shows how Hebble was a stepping stone for management material with the average age of the General Managers being in the early 30s when they joined the Company then progressing up the ladder.

In 1946 Hebble received its first delivery of postwar chassis: 12 AEC Regals with Weymann bodies replaced the ailing Albions, which had done the bulk of the work during the war. A further 15 Regals were delivered the following year but with Roe bodies.

That same year, 1947, saw the sale by Thomas Tilling to the British Transport Commission of all their financial interests in the bus companies they were associated with, for £24.8 million. This brought about proposals for Area Boards with the first one being suggested for the North East. Such was the objection made by the operators including the municipalities that the schemes were not proceeded with. Later all the road operators, both passenger and goods, owned by the Government were placed under a separate organisation called the Transport Holding Company. None of this affected Hebble as the nearest THC operator was West Yorkshire with whom they had a good working relationship.

While Hebble were receiving new buses the Ministry of Supply had placed a ban on the manufacture of coach bodies from 31st March

Hebble's fleet number **3** (**CP 9538**) was a Leyland LT3 Lion with 32 bus seats in a Leyland-built front-entrance body. New in August 1931, it was one of a batch of four purchased by the railway-owned Hebble company, all of which were transferred to Yorkshire (WD) in June 1932 when Hebble became a BET subsidiary - presumably because they were not Albions. Number 3 passed to the War Department in July 1940 and was not returned to YWD. This form of the fleetname transfer appeared during railway ownership, reverting to the original afterwards. *(Both: John Banks Collection)*

>> *Opposite page:* The Albion PMA28 shown on page 7 battling its way through snowdrifts is seen here when newly rebodied by Eastern Counties, having lost its Ramsden coach body. Number **120** (**CP 7578**), after withdrawal in 1946, was sold to an operator in Holloway, London. *(Senior Transport Archive)*

1948. This seemed to apply to the bigger coachbuilders, in order that they could concentrate on bus bodies, and not the small body builders who had sprung up after the war. The BET Board suggested that any coach bodies which could not be completed to their original specifications be changed to single-deck service-bus type.

Hebble had received three Leyland PS1 Tigers with Windover bodies in 1948 and this ban may account for no more coaches being received until three years later. Then, just to add to the problems, the Government made a cut of 12½% on fuel available for private hire operation.

Hebble's first concern, like that of most companies, was that stage carriage routes should return to prewar level and were inclined not to operate excursions and tours. This brought problems when in August 1948 they had objected to an application by J Hoyle and Sons to add three additional excursion destinations to Bradford, Leeds and Manchester for football matches and theatre visits. Hebble stated that the stage carriage services could be duplicated to meet the public demand but also agreed they were not operating any vehicles under their excursion licence from Halifax.

The Chairman of the Yorkshire Traffic Commissioners, Major Eastwood, had a quiet word with W J James, a BET Director, on the fact that it was hard to sustain an objection when you were not operating a similar excursion although holding a licence. This brought instructions from the various Chairmen to their companies that a reasonable programme of excursions should be operated where licences were held to minimise the risk of other operators being licensed and so establishing themselves as competitors.

Each company associated with the BET was a member of the BET Federation, which had been formed in 1907 to negotiate bulk purchases for the BET Tramway and Electric Companies, and also offered technical, legal and secretarial

services. This was expanded to the newly formed bus companies and included such things as tyre testing, fuel comparisons, testing of different chassis makes and designs of bus bodies.

The BET did not force any of its subsidiaries to purchase a certain chassis or body, this was left to each individual operator, but in the case of Hebble the saving on a chassis or body could be considerable when added on to orders for other companies.

Hebble paid a yearly sum to the Federation for the engineering and secretarial services provided and received each month details of their omnibus expenditure per car mile operated. Out of the 31 companies involved Hebble seemed to stick around the 12th position in performance throughout the 1950s. This compared well with other smaller units such as County Motors or Stratford Blue. During this period approximately 40% of Hebble's total mileage was operated by double-deck vehicles.

In 1952 a merger of routes took place with the Yorkshire (WD) Company whereby the Hebble Halifax - Wyke route was linked to the Wyke - Cleckheaton route of Yorkshire (WD) to form a jointly operated through service. A further two joint services, between Cleckheaton - Scholes and Cleckheaton - Windy Bank, were also introduced. In all cases receipts were pooled and a monthly settlement was made on the basis of mileage operated at a common rate per mile.

In 1953 a new issue of 90,000 £1 shares, based on three new shares for every two shares held, was floated. These were taken up by BET and the railways.

Nineteen-fifty-four saw an increase in the coach fleet by four Leyland Royal Tigers with Bellhouse Hartwell bodies. They had been intended for the Blue Cars Continental Cruises fleet, but after that firm had been purchased by the BET the year before the vehicles had been diverted to Hebble who portrayed them on the front of the timetable and in private hire

23

Above: Number **90** (**CP 9837**), an Albion Victor PH49 with Weymann 20-seat bodywork. New in June 1932, it was withdrawn in 1939 and passed to Young's, of Paisley, thence to Bere Regis & District, who withdrew it in 1945. *(Hebble Collection)*

Below: Number **93** (**JX 500**) was another Albion Victor PH49, this time with with Eastern Counties 20-seat bodywork. One of a March 1933 batch of three, it was sold in 1939 and used by an independent operator until 1949. *(Senior Transport Archive)*

>> *Opposite page:* The interior, looking to the rear, of the Eastern Counties bodywork on No. **93** (**JX 500**). These small Albions were driver-only operated. *(Senior Transport Archive)*

advertising as the pride of the fleet. By the end of the year the Hebble fleet consisted of 83 vehicles: 46 single-deckers, 19 double-deckers and 18 coaches.

The withdrawal of the railway service from Halifax via Queensbury to Bradford saw Hebble applying for rail replacement services between Wilsden (New Inn) and Cullingworth (Mill Street) and a second, circular, route from Town Gate, Clayton, Bradford. These commenced in May 1955 on a three month trial but continued until withdrawn three years later. Like most rail replacements they carried few passengers and cost too much to run.

The last delivery of lowbridge double-deckers took place in 1956, these being two AEC Regent Vs with Weymann Orion bodies. The year also brought in late December the Suez Crisis, as it became known, with fuel being rationed again and reductions having to be made in the frequency of services. The tax on fuel was also increased on 4th December by 1/- per gallon with further increases on 6th of 2d per gallon and the 19th by 3d a gallon. To meet these increases bus companies were given dispensation to make a 12½% increase in fares while the emergency lasted. It was not until April 1957 that the restrictions on fuel were lifted although not all services returned to their pre-Suez frequency. However, the Government did not remove all the fuel tax so, to cover the loss, when the 12½% dispensation finished Hebble applied for a 12½% increase in fares to commence the following day.

This was not the end of that year's problems: a nationwide strike by the staff of BET and THC bus companies, plus those of the larger Independents, took place between 20th and 28th July; then in September the country was hit by a flu epidemic which caused not only a drop in passengers carried but cuts in services because of staff illness.

An unusual application was made by James Johnson of Bradford to operate a service from Bradford to Halifax (Greyhound Stadium) every Tuesday and Friday for the conveyance of passengers and their dogs. Although Hebble and Halifax objected on the grounds of their services operating between the two towns it was rather a light-hearted one because of the dogs and a licence was granted for six months limited to one vehicle.

Excursions, tours and express services

Hebble, as will be seen, was principally a bus operator, but it was unable to expand or introduce any new routes, and its stage carriage operation had reached its peak in the 1950s: thus they had to look for expansion in other directions. Apart from the involvement in the Yorkshire - Blackpool Pool and a service to Scarborough, all other long-distance services from their area were operated by associated companies and, except for vehicles being hired as duplicates, Hebble had no real involvement in them.

They did run a very successful travel agency in Halifax and one operator they booked for was Yelloway Motor Services, of Rochdale, who operated a daily service to Torquay from that town. A close working relationship had been set up between the two Companies going back to the 1930s when the early morning 28 service from Halifax to Rochdale (Smith Street) made connections with Yelloway just around the corner in Weir Street. This arrangement included offering holidays in Torquay from Halifax with the cost including coach travel, hotel accommodation and excursions at the resort. Other destinations were also available by changing at Cheltenham.

After the Second World War the booking facility for the Yelloway Devonian service continued but inclusive holidays were not offered. The demand for travel increased each year and by 1955 had reached the position where Hebble were operating through coaches from Bradford and Halifax across Rochdale to Torquay on hire to Yelloway and also to Bournemouth and Southsea via Cheltenham for Associated Motorways. For example, to meet the demand for the 1955 Halifax Wakes Week Hebble provided four vehicles for the Friday night service to the South-West but they also had to hire another twelve vehicles from Yelloway to cover the advance bookings made from Halifax. A similar situation would arise on the Saturday morning.

Yorkshire operators were looking at the traffic going to Torquay and for the next two years there was to be a series of applications by various operators for services to that resort. To protect themselves Hebble, jointly with Yelloway, applied for two routes during this period, the first from Bradford to Torquay via Halifax and Huddersfield which was refused. The second made later for Halifax to Torquay was also refused by the Traffic Commissioners.

Hebble then applied for an additional express route between Bradford and Halifax to Rochdale (Weir Street) for pre-booked passengers to connect with the Yelloway service and after several refusals it was eventually granted.

Some three years after the original applications Wallace Arnold, J W Kitchin and Hansons were each granted a limited licence to Torquay for the holiday periods of Leeds, Bradford and Huddersfield respectively - one town to each operator.

Meanwhile, Hebble continued to operate across Rochdale on hire to Yelloway as required. Other through-running facilities were offered including seaside resorts in North Wales as far as Llandudno again via Rochdale but in conjunction with the Yelloway subsidiary Creams. Morecambe and Southport were covered by the Hebble service 15 to Burnley connecting there with Ribble services to Southport (X5) and Morecambe (X14). During the summer months through vehicles were operated by Hebble on Saturdays. Through bookings were also available via Squires Gate Airport, Blackpool for the Isle of Man and Ireland. Later the Channel Islands were included and all these helped to increase revenue.

The day and half day excursion market was something else that could be expanded and in 1954 the Halifax firm of Brearleys Tours was purchased; five vehicles were taken over and immediately sold on.

Other operators also had the idea of expanding. Halifax Corporation, like most municipalities, held excursion & tours licences to operate local tours within the boundaries of the borough. Hebble did not object to them as long as they were contained within the municipal boundary even though they held similar licences.

In 1955 a series of applications by the Halifax JOC for licences to operate tours from Illingworth, Brighouse and Sowerby Bridge as well as extending the Halifax licences saw Hebble together with eight other local operators making objections to the proposals. Firstly, they objected to Halifax applying for consent to run public service vehicles along roads which were not within the municipal boundary; they also lodged objections to the proposed excursions and thirdly made application for similar tours to those proposed by the JOC if they did not already have them on their licence.

The strength of the combined objections was so great that the Traffic Commissioners refused to grant consent to Halifax to run outside the borough which meant Halifax JOC had to withdraw their applications. However, the Traffic Commissioners also refused the new tours requested by the coach operators as well just to maintain the status quo.

In 1957 the excursion business of Ripponden & District was purchased and this included the firm of Weightman Tours, which had been merged with Ripponden a few years earlier. Eleven vehicles were included, six of which were Commer Avengers, a type of chassis not seen in the Hebble fleet since the 1930s. This brought new picking-up points at Ripponden and Hebden Bridge.

The following year saw the purchase of Walton and Halliwell which was an associate of O & C Holdsworth and apart from excursion licences they also operated a service to Great Yarmouth. The fleet comprised an assortment of Bedfords of which six SBG models with Duple Super Vega bodies were retained.

The appointment of Frank Woodworth as Traffic Manager to the Company occurred in 1958. Prior to 1953 he had been with the East Kent Road Car Company where he had been responsible for Continental Tour operations, and from 1953 to 1958 had been involved with two new companies purchased by BET: Blue Car Continental Tours and Red Line Motorways, both based in London.

His first job on arrival at Hebble was to amalgamate the various excursion licences held by them and by 1960 there were twenty five picking-up points and 186 separate destinations were licensed. Period returns during the annual Wakes Weeks were also available to Skegness, Cleethorpes and Llandudno. In order to attract passengers the Company advertised "Five ways in Five days", this was based on five different day excursions, which included lunch and tea. Passengers booked for the whole five days and had the same seat each day and in many cases the same driver. Two- and three-day tour licences were obtained with London being a popular destination, and there were inclusive holidays in Blackpool and the Isle of Man.

In the holiday periods the daily allowance on excursion and tours was 68 vehicles. During an appeal heard between Hebble and J B Sheard t/a James Hoyle & Son, where Sheard had applied to increase their small vehicle allowance on excursions, Hebble objected, stating that they had a right to fill all their 68 vehicles before any other operators should be granted additional vehicles.

This big brother attitude by Hebble did not go down well with the Inspector hearing the appeal and he could not agree with their argument especially as Hebble could only meet half their allowance with their own vehicles and the Company had given no indication of intending to add to their fleet of luxury coaches. The Inspector felt that on excursions there was a certain amount of loyalty for one operator as against the other, in this case Sheards as against Hebble. Hebble lost the appeal.

The position was fast approaching where the excursions and private hire were sustaining the stage carriage routes which in some cases were beginning to operate at a loss.

The final BET years 1960 - 1968

In 1961 new lightweight coaches were purchased to replace the Bedfords. These were Ford Thames with Duple Yeoman bodies and further Fords were purchased a few years later.

At the financial year ending 31st March 1963 Hebble had a fleet of 80 vehicles consisting of 22 double-deckers, nine single-deckers, 21 one-man vehicles and 28 coaches; the overall seating capacity was 3,845. It had operated 3,159,377 miles in the year, carried 10,120,225 passengers and made a net profit before tax of £37,288 on gross receipts of £402,436. There were 15 stage carriage routes of which 14 were run on a daily basis, the odd one being the "Wibsey Flyer" which still ran on Saturdays only. Seven of these routes were operated from Halifax depot, Bradford had five routes with a further three operated jointly by the two depots. In addition to the daily operation there were also schools and works services plus excursions, private hire and express services.

The coach fleet now represented over one third of the vehicles owned.

Frank Woodworth became General Manager of the Company in the same year and was then borrowed by the BET Board a few years later to do a report on the viability of his old company, Red Line Continental. Although on the basis of the report the company was given one more chance it was finally wound up in 1968 with Hebble receiving another vehicle, this time a Red Line AEC with a Duple Continental body.

In 1964 Norman Dean, as General Manager of Yorkshire Traction representing the Yorkshire Services Pool, met with Malcolm Barr of Wallace Arnold and Hubert Allen of Yelloway Motor Services to try and put together a scheme of services to serve the South West of England rather than the linking arrangements that prevailed at this time.

A joint application was lodged by Associated Motorways, Yorkshire Services Pool, Wallace Arnold, J W Kitchin, Yelloway and Hebble to operate daily from Yorkshire to Cheltenham and Torquay. After a series of Traffic Court hearings spread over eighteen months, licences were granted although only for the summer months to begin with and the service known as the "South West Clipper" commenced on 1st May, 1967.

Hebble now gave up their through-booking facility with Yelloway, this being replaced by the two companies operating direct from Yorkshire on the Clipper routes.

There were two interesting additions to the fleet. In 1966 the first rear-engined double-decker, a Daimler Fleetline with a Northern Counties body, was delivered. Two years later four AEC Reliances with Duple Northern Dragonfly bodies were transferred from the Samuelsons fleet in London. Only six Dragonfly bodies were ever built.

One town that was not linked directly to Halifax by bus was Todmorden, for which passengers had to change at Hebden Bridge. A four-part through return ticket had been available between the two towns, at least in 1949. The ticket carried the names of Todmorden JOC, Halifax JOC and Hebble, and was available on any of the operators' vehicles. How long this was in use is not known, but in 1967 Halifax and Todmorden JOC commenced a joint through service between the two towns

Above: Number **98** (**JX 505**) was the third of a batch of three Albion PW65s with Brush 32-seat bodies new in March 1933. It was withdrawn in 1945, joined the fleet of an independent and was scrapped in 1952. The photograph was taken in Karrier Street, Halifax. *(Alan Cross Collection/J F Higham)*

Below: In May 1933 Hebble bought two Albion PV70 models fitted with English Electric 28-seat coach bodies. One of them, No. **99** (**JX 506**) is seen outside the Granby Hotel, Queensbury. The fleetname was enclosed in a garter, which was the fashion for coaches in the 1930s. JX 506 was withdrawn in 1949 and saw further service with a fairground showman. *(Senior Transport Archive)*

principally to serve the Calder Valley High School for which, previously, school children had had to change vehicle *en route*. Although Hebble objected mainly on the grounds that they should also be included in the operation, because of their Halifax - Hebden Bridge link, the application was granted to the two Joint Omnibus Committees.

One of the first Directors of Hebble in 1932 had been 28-year old John Spencer Wills who, a few years later, became Chairman of the Company. He progressed up the ladder of promotion with the BET and became Managing Director in 1946, a position he held until the death of Harold Drayton in 1966, when Wills became Chairman as well as MD. The following year he had the task of informing his Board that the time had come to sell their bus interests to the Government. Thus, on 1st March 1968 the British Electric Traction together with its subsidiary companies sold all their financial interests in their various bus companies in the United Kingdom to the Transport Holding Company for £46.9 million. Not all of it went to the BET group as there were still a lot of individual shareholders, even in the companies where the railways held shares equal to the BET: in Southdown Motor Services, for example, 33.8% of the shares were held by private shareholders.

At a meeting of BET General Managers held on 27th June 1968, A F R Carling, chairing the meeting, referred to the purchase of the group by the THC stating that THC did not propose to alter the company structure of the provincial bus industry, but as in recent cases of the Hebble and Mexborough companies, some of the smaller companies might, however, be placed within the management structure of a neighbouring larger company. This referred to the General Manager of Yorkshire (WD) taking on additional responsibility for Hebble from 1st March after Frank Woodworth became General Manager of South Wales Transport: thus were Hebble's days numbered.

Another factor was the purchase by THC on 1st January of that year of West Riding Automobile Services. They had started as a Tramway Company in 1905 known as the Yorkshire (West Riding) Electric Tramway Company Ltd gradually changing to motor buses over the years and adopting the present

title in 1935. As at the time of their purchase West Riding operated over 400 vehicles, where would it fit into the overall picture?

A new start - the National Bus Company 1969 - 1974

On 1st January 1969, the National Bus Company was formed to amalgamate the former THC and BET companies plus the assets of the railways in the Joint Omnibus Committees. This led to the introduction later in the year of four Passenger Transport Authorities to take over the municipal bus operations within their areas and also to work closely with the NBC companies in the areas formed. It would be a few more years before that would happen in Yorkshire with the introduction of Metropolitan Counties on 1st April 1974.

With the formation of the NBC and the transfer of the railway interests in bus operation a separate company was formed to take over the railway operation. Known as Amalgamated Passenger Transport Ltd, abbreviated to APT, it had its head office at Saville Town, Dewsbury and later transferred to Belle Isle, Wakefield. The Company had been formed on 8th April 1967 by the renaming of a THC dormant company registered in 1929 as the Midland National Omnibus Company Ltd. The share capital of APT was 100 £1 shares of which seven were issued.

By the end of 1969 it had sold its interest in the Huddersfield JOC to that Corporation and negotiations were ongoing to do the same at Sheffield. APT's investments at that time in the three remaining Committees - Sheffield, Todmorden and Halifax - amounted to £555,012. The APT name replaced that of the railways on the sides of certain vehicles as the registered owner.

So where did Hebble fit in all this? It did mean closer working with Yorkshire (WD), taking over the Halifax - Cleckheaton - Leeds route, together with some vehicles and also combining the Halifax - Bingley routes with the Yorkshire (WD) Ossett - Keighley service although Hebble vehicles did not reach the latter town. Hebble also took over Yorkshire Woollen District's responsibilities on three joint services. The Park Avenue depot at Bradford which had replaced Ederthorpe Street in 1943 was closed

Above: **JX 1407** was an Albion PW67, new in May 1934, which had Brush 32-seat bodywork and was allocated Hebble fleet number **110**. Fitted with a diesel engine from new, it was withdrawn in 1940 and passed into Royal Air Force use.

Below: Brush coachwork of the early 1930s was to a high standard of appointments and comfort, as evidenced by this view looking towards the rear in Hebble No. **6** (**CP 9830**), an Albion PWJ dating from June 1932. Another 1945 withdrawal it, too, passed to a travelling fairground showman. *(Both: Senior Transport Archive)*

and the vehicles were moved to the West Yorkshire depot in Hammerton Street.

This was followed on 1st May 1970 with a complete change in the role of Hebble. The coaching activities of Yorkshire (WD) were transferred to Hebble including licences from the North-East to Liverpool and Coventry, as well as Yorkshire to London and the South Coast. Their share in the Yorkshire - Blackpool and all excursions and tours licences were also transferred plus a total of 46 coaches including six which were on order, thus bringing the fleet to approximately 130 vehicles.

One route transferred was the X12 Bradford - Manchester service operated jointly with North Western Road Car. On summer Saturdays the service was linked to the North Western service from Manchester to Llandudno and Hebble vehicles could be seen operating across Manchester to North Wales on a regular Saturday basis. There were changes also in the Bradford area where on 3rd May the services to Bingley and Huddersfield were transferred to West Yorkshire.

The APT involvement in the Halifax JOC continued and discussions were taking place between Halifax and the NBC on the future of Hebble. On 21st February 1971 the Hebble services from Halifax to Leeds via Dudley Hill and to Cleckheaton via Wyke as well as the two services to Burnley and Rochdale passed to the Halifax JOC. On 1st March all the remaining stage carriage routes, with a few exceptions, were transferred to the JOC together with a number of vehicles: four went to Halifax Corporation and nine to Halifax JOC, a total of 13 - exactly the same number as in the 1929 transfer. The Leeds - Halifax via Cleckheaton route reverted back to Yorkshire (WD) as did also the Hebble interest in the Sheffield White Rose Service which had commenced in 1969. The Bradford - Manchester service also returned to Yorkshire (WD) although by February the following year it would be licensed to West Riding Automobile.

In June application was made by the Halifax JOC to take over from Hebble certain excursions, mostly half-day or afternoon and evening circulars, which were licensed to them from Mytholmroyd, Sowerby Bridge, Mixenden, Ripponden, Elland, Hebden Bridge and Halifax.

On 2nd August the retirement of the General Manager of Todmorden JOC brought about a merger of the two JOCs with the Halifax General Manager being responsible for both and they were renamed as the Calderdale Joint Omnibus Committee. The APT was still a 50% partner with an investment worth £164,336.

By now the General Manager of the West Riding Automobile had retired and the Yorkshire (WD) General Manager had the added responsibility of this Company in addition to Hebble. The three Companies became the West Riding Group because of the area served.

The Hebble coach fleet was moved to the former Yorkshire (WD) garage at Frost Hill, Liversedge, and Walnut Street was closed. By 1st April Hebble had become an all coach fleet of 61 vehicles and for the next two years was the coaching arm of the West Riding Group.

The ending of the Hebble stage carriage operations was considered by many as the end of the Company but, as will be seen in the next chapter, it still had a role to play.

National Travel 1974 - 1988

Freddie Wood, the Chairman of the National Bus Company, had always been a fan of the Greyhound Lines of America from the time he lived and worked in the United States and had a vision of a similar organisation in Britain.

With this in mind the Central Activities Group had been set up under David Glassborow to explore the possibilities amongst other ideas. This led to the formation of a Company called National Travel (NBC) Ltd which was to control and promote all express service activities. In 1973 five areas were set up under National Travel being Midlands, South West, South East, North West and North East regions.

The following year limited companies were formed by renaming what were originally coach concerns in the various areas, with Hebble becoming National Travel (North East) Ltd.

This meant that there was a coach fleet allocated to each region which was not under the control of a bus company and could be built on in the future. As far as the public were concerned the only change to begin with was that all the coaches were now painted all-over white with National on the side and a very small

Above: One of a batch of six Northern Counties-bodied lowbridge 51-seat Leyland TD4 Titans new in April 1935. The batch was registered JX 2534-9 and had fleet numbers 121-6. All were rebodied during the Second World War and five passed to Yorkshire Traction in 1949. *(Hebble Collection)*

Below: Under construction at the coachbuilding factory of Charles H Roe in 1937 is seen the last of a batch of four Leyland TD5 Titans with 53-seat lowbridge bodywork. All were withdrawn in 1949 and this one - No. **153** (**JX 5731**) - ran for an independent until 1952 and was scrapped in 1954. *(Senior Transport Archive)*

Above: New in April 1935, No. **127** (**JX 2540**) was one of a pair of Albion SpPW67s with Roe 32-seat bodywork. It worked for Hebble until withdrawal and sale in 1946, after which it operated for an independent until 1949.

Below: In April 1936 three new Albion SpPW69s were delivered. Again with Roe bodywork, they had Gardner 5LW diesel engines. All were sold to Sheffield United Tours in 1946, and then to a dealer in 1949. This one, No. **130** (**JX 3591**), is known to have run for a showman between 1959 and 1961. The blind is set for the Todmorden to Scarborough service. The drop-down "DUPLICATE" flap was peculiar in Yorkshire, and possibly the whole country, to Hebble and Yorkshire (WD) District. *(Both: Senior Transport Archive)*

Above: Number **146** (**JX 4719**) was a 1937 Albion SpPW141, one of six delivered in March of that year. Bodywork was by Roe and again Gardner 5LW engines were specified from new. All were withdrawn in 1947 and scrapped the following year.

Below: The last of a trio of January 1939 Albion CX11s, No. **158** (**JX 6891**) is seen in the snow outside Charles H Roe's premises prior to delivery to Hebble. The Gardner 5LW was once more the power unit chosen. This vehicle was withdrawn in 1950 and sold to a local building contractor for use as a site hut. *(Both: Senior Transport Archive)*

fleet name. Also, if they had taken any notice in the past, the route numbers were changed from the familiar X on most routes to three numbers and all routes in the North-East region were allocated in the 200/300 series. Gradually, the express services in the area were relicensed to National Travel (North East) from the original operators, who also assumed responsibility for the Sheffield United Tours operation and fleet. This would later become the basis for the National Holidays organisation.

In 1976 National Travel (NBC) received a new Director and Controller, E G Davies, who had been Hebble General Manager from 1958 to 1963.

A further change of name occurred in 1977 when National Travel (Midlands) was split between the North West and the North East companies and to cover its new area North East became National Travel (East) Ltd.

According to official records the Company became dormant on 9th September 1979 when control of express services and their operation was transferred back to National Travel (NBC) who then formed National Express Regions with all the coaches coming under National Travel (NBC). This really was the end of the Company as an operator although the fleetname National Travel (East) keeps occurring over the next few years.

During the previous years it had reorganised the holiday tour programmes by combining the tours operated by various NBC companies throughout England into one product - National Holidays. Although problems were encountered at the beginning with low bookings and tours being cancelled, National Holidays became a firm favourite with the travel industry, winning many awards over the years.

October 1980 saw the first round of deregulation taking place with licences no longer required for express services and excursions and tours. Licences still had to be applied for if passengers were picked up and set down on the same journey within 30 miles of the commencement of their journey.

When National Travel (NBC) was broken up again in 1984, the coaches in the East Region were transferred to the West Riding Group who again set up a coach operation. National Express, National Holidays and National Travelworld were passed to National Products. When road service licences were required for parts of express services to meet the revised licensing conditions they were applied for by another National Product member, London Country Bus Services, trading as National Express East Region. This was until National Express obtained their own "O" Licence together with four vehicles, so they could licence services in their own name.

In 1986 the Frost Hill garage was closed and sold for £130,000. The same year saw the commencement of the break-up of the National Bus Company and the public sale of all the companies to meet the privatisation regulations. In 1987 84 coaches plus property were sold to A T Lavin for £750,000 but from further information it looks like £660,000 was the purchase price. Lavin, to control the various coach companies he had purchased, formed ATL Holdings with a subsidiary company called NTE Coaches Ltd to take over part of the West Riding Coaching interests. NTE was later changed to SUT.

The dormant National Travel (East) Ltd was finally wound up by NBC in the following year so ending the link going back to 1924.

A former Traffic Manager of Hebble who went on to higher things remarked to the writer, some twenty odd years ago, that the removal by NBC of small companies such as Hebble meant that newcomers into the industry on management level did not have the opportunity to test their skills and find their feet before being placed with a larger company. He had learnt a lot at Hebble and this had always stood him in good stead in later years. Perhaps that says it all about the company - it is as good an epitaph as any.

Above: Number **147** (**JX 5785**), the first of three 35-seat Eastern Coach Works-bodied Albion SpPW141 models, fitted with Gardner 5LW engines, that were new in January 1938. All were scrapped in 1948 after withdrawal from service the previous year. Similar bodywork from ECW graced the last batch of new Albions bought by Hebble on CX11 chassis in May 1940. *(Senior Transport Archive)*

Below: Number **159** (**JX 7337**) was one of two Albion CX9s, new in 1939 with Roe bodywork and Albion EN234A diesel engines. Both were withdrawn in December 1950 and this one was sold to a local builder for use as a site hut. *(John Banks Collection)*

Hebble in Scarborough in the prewar period

Demand for vehicles for express work, private hire and excursions was such both before and after the war that Hebble often used buses when necessary and some were even painted in coach livery *(see page 44 lower)*. Number **107** (**JX 1404**) - a vehicle similar in specification to that illustrated and described on page 31 *(upper)* - is seen parked on the promenade *(above)* and No. **139** (**JX 4712**)was parked in Vine Street garage. This was an Albion PK115 fitted with an Albion EN212B four-cylinder petrol engine and a Duple 26-seat coach body. It had been new in March 1937 and remained with Hebble until 1950. *(Both: W J Haynes Collection/G H F Atkins)*

Above: Leyland Titan TD5 No. **161** (**JX 7991**) was the first of a pair bodied as lowbridge 53-seaters by Eastern Coach Works and new in January 1940. It was withdrawn in 1952 and after service with a subsequent owner was scrapped in 1964. The 29 Bradford to Halifax via Wibsey service, introduced in 1934, throughout its existence ran only on Saturdays. A round trip could be done in just under an hour and the service became known as "the Wibsey Flyer".

Below: Number **171** (**JX 8361**) was one of two Leyland TD7 Titans new in 1942 and fitted with Roe utility bodywork built to a design specified by the Ministry of Supply. The lowbridge 53-seater is seen in New Road, Halifax, and was withdrawn in 1953. It was last licensed, to a private owner, as a horsebox as late as 1961. *(Both: D Akrigg Collection)*

Above: Originally fitted with a Burlingham body when new in 1936, Leyland Titan TD4 No. **134** (**JX 3595**) was rebodied with utility lowbridge 53-seat bodywork by Northern Coachbuilders in 1944. It was photographed in Chester Street bus station prior to departing for Halifax on route 17. This bus was sold to Yorkshire Traction in 1949, then to a dealer. It ended up with a private owner as a hen hut. *(D Akrigg Collection)*

Below: Number **173** (**JX 8456**) was a wartime Guy Arab II 6LW, supplied in 1944 fitted with a Strachans 55-seat lowbridge body built to austerity standards. In 1949 it was rebodied by Roe as a 53-seater, again lowbridge. In 1952 it passed to the Potteries Motor Traction Company via a dealer and remained in service until 1959. It is illustrated in King Street, Leeds, with its 1949 Roe body. *(W J Haynes)*

Above: The first postwar buses, delivered in the second half of 1946, were a batch of twelve AEC Regal 0662s with Weymann 35-seat bodywork. They had fleet numbers 179-90 and were registered JX 9104-15. Number **181** (**JX 9106**) is seen in rural surroundings *en route* to Bradford on route 19 from Bingley via Harden and Wilsden on 24th April 1954. Converted to a lorry in 1956, the vehicle was withdrawn in 1970, sold into preservation and still exists.

Below: Number **184** (**JX 9109**) of the same batch is seen in Buttershaw on route 25 from Bradford on 20th March 1955. It was withdrawn in 1956, sold to a dealer, and scrapped in 1959. *(Both: D Akrigg Collection/J Copland)*

Above: Number **2** (**GRR 312**) was the second of two Weymann-bodied 32-seat Leyland PS1 Tigers acquired in 1947 from East Midland Motor Services, who had licensed but never operated them. They started a new Hebble fleet numbering sequence and initially ran in East Midland livery with Hebble fleetname transfers. The vehicle is seen at the King Street terminus in Leeds, apparently working as a duplicate, as vehicles leaving Leeds usually showed Rochdale or Burnley as the destination. *(John Banks Collection/G H F Atkins)*

Below: One of two Leyland PS1/1 Tigers new in 1947, No. **6** (**JX 9734**) was originally fitted with a 1936 Burlingham coach body taken from a 1930 chassis. It was rebodied as shown with a Windover 35-seat fully fronted coach body in 1952 and is seen in Blackpool. It was sold to a dealer in 1959 and ran for two subsequent owners until 1964. *(Geoff Coxon)*

Upper: The other 1947 Leyland PS1/1 *(see previous page)* was No. **7** (**JX 9735**). When new it carried a 1937 Duple 30 seat coach body taken from a 1929 Leyland TS2 Tiger *(illustrated on page 17 upper fitted with its original body)*. Number 7 was also rebodied in 1952 with a Windover fully fronted body. Withdrawn in 1959, it had three subsequent owners, one of whom modified the front as shown. *(D Akrigg Collection/C W Routh)*

Centre: Number **5** (**JX 9818**) was the last of three 1948 Windover-bodied 31-seat Leyland PS1/1 Tigers. In the 1957 renumbering it became No. 13 (nobody supersitious at Hebble) and was withdrawn in 1959. *(Geoff Coxon)*

Lower: Number **8** (**JX 9819**) was the first of a batch of 15 1947 AEC Regal 0662 models fitted with Roe 32-seat bodies. It was photographed in the yard at the Gibbet Street end of the Halifax depot. The picture was taken with a 24s/6d Kodak "Brownie": a good camera if the subject was stationary, the photographer had a steady hand and the sun was shining. The vehicle was withdrawn in 1959 and passed via a dealer to a contractor. *(Nicholas Harris)*

Above: Number **11** (**JX 9822**) was another of the batch of 15 1947 AEC Regals *(see page 43)*. This one was withdrawn in 1957 and presumably scrapped, as there is no trace of any relicensing. *(Senior Transport Archive)*

Below: Number **24** (**ACP 724**) was the middle vehicle of a batch of three 1948 Weymann-bodied 32-seat Leyland PS1 Tigers. Unlike the other two vehicles in the batch, this one carried coach livery for many years for use on express services, excursions and private hire *(see page 38)*. It is seen leaving Leeds on Wellington Street bound for Rochdale on route 28. Behind the car is the old Leeds coach station with the booking office on the right. Wellington Street coach station closed when the new Dyer Street premises opened: the old site was subsequently redeveloped. Leaving the picture on the right is a 1939 ECW-bodied Bristol L6G coach of the West Yorkshire Road Car Company. *(Geoff Coxon)*

>> *Opposite page:* Hebble's first postwar double-decker was No. **26** (**AJX 241**). It was one of a batch of five AEC Regent 9612Es with 53-seat Roe lowbridge bodywork. Number 26 was new in November 1948 and is seen on route 18, which ran from Bingley to Duckworth Lane, on 23rd June 1957. The bus was withdrawn in 1959 and survived with a Scottish independent until 1961. *(D Akrigg Collection/J Copland)*

<< *Opposite page:* The last batch of AEC Regent III 9621E models was delivered in 1950 as Nos 44-6 (BJX 55-7). They again had Roe 53-seat lowbridge bodywork. The middle one of the three, after renumbering as **245** (**BJX 56**), is seen on the Bradford to Bingley route 19 on 6th August 1961. It was withdrawn in 1962. *(D Akrigg Collection/J Copland)*

This page: The AEC Regents in traffic - representatives of two batches in two angles of the same Chester Street scene. Note the improved destination blind layout on the newer vehicle and that the setts and the tram lines had disappeared when the road was resurfaced. Numbers **28** (**AJX 243**) and **35** (**BCP 248**) are the buses, with Yorkshire Traction, Yorkshire (WD) and West Yorkshire vehicles also visible. *(D Akrigg Collection/ R F Mack; D Akrigg Collection/J Copland)*

Above: Another view of No. **24** (**ACP 724**) in coach livery, taken on 12th July 1953 at Union Street South, Halifax. Note the destination blind, which did not need changing between journeys. Route 40 was operated jointly with Yorkshire (WD). The vehicle was withdrawn in 1959 and passed via a dealer to a contractor. *(D Akrigg Collection/J Copland)*

Below: BCP 825-30 were the most renumbered vehicles in the Hebble fleet. Willowbrook-bodied Leyland PS2/3 Tigers, they were new in 1950 and carried fleet numbers 38-43, 16-21, 181-6 and 130-5 in turn. Note the Hebble AEC Regal on the right and that all the vehicles visible in this Scarborough picture are halfcabs. The BCPs were later repainted into bus livery and were withdrawn in 1962, **BCP 826** (fleet number **39** in our picture and therefore fairly new) being another to end up as transport for a building contractor. These buses - 33-seaters - were an unfortunate buy for Hebble, for very soon afterwards underfloor-engined vehicles with a seating capacity of around 43 became widely available. *(John Banks Collection/G H F Atkins)*

Eight vehicles were acquired from Yorkshire (WD) in 1950 and were sold in 1951. None was repainted into Hebble livery but they were given Hebble fleetname transfers. Number **194** (**HD 6606**) *(above)* was an Eastern Coach Works-bodied Leyland TS8 Tiger. It is seen leaving Chester Street bus station, Bradford, on 1st August 1950, for Bingley on route 19. Number **197** (**HD 6610**), a similar vehicle, is seen *(below)* at the Mountain terminus of route 11 to Duckworth Lane on 21st April 1951. The chassis of No. 194 was subsequently exported to the Gold Coast and No. 197 later worked for a building contractor. *(Both: D Akrigg Collection/J Copland)*

Above: In 1951 Hebble received its first underfloor-engined vehicles, Nos 47-52 (BJX 675-80), Leyland PSU1/9 Royal Tigers with Willowbrook 43-seat bodies. When new they carried coach livery, demonstrated by No. **47** (**BJX 675**) at Scarborough. *(John Banks Collection/G H F Atkins)*

Below: After repainting into service bus livery in the late 1950s the Royal Tigers were still used for services to the coast. Renumbered No. **151** (**BJX 679**) was so employed in Blackpool. These buses were withdrawn in 1963 (BJX 675) and 1964. *(A D Jack)*

Below and >>>page 53: A batch of six Leyland PSU1/15 Royal Tigers with Leyland 41-seat coach bodies was delivered in 1951 [2] and 1952 [4]. Number **56** (**CCP 226**) is seen when brand new outside church and hostelry. It was withdrawn at the end of the 1965 summer season and passed via a dealer to the contractor George Wimpey. *(John Banks Collection)*

The interior of the Leyland Royal Tiger coaches was soldily reassuring and the vehicles gave a comfortable ride. With the entrance between the axles, the body could accommodate a double seat in the front-nearside corner, alongside the driver: a particularly exciting place to be for the caption writer, who was a schoolboy when these coaches were new. *(Both: John Banks Collection)*

This page: In 1953 eight Leyland Royal Tigers of type PSU1/13 with Weymann 44-seat bodies were delivered. Originally painted in coach livery, they were later repainted as buses. The Company experienced difficulties in keeping the reversed livery clean and the cream tended to fade, thus when panels had to be replaced the vehicles took on a blotchy appearance. Number **66** (**CJX 67**) was photographed *(above)* in King Street, Leeds and *(below)* No. **163** (**CJX 64**) was turning into Rhodesway on the way from Duckworth Lane to Queensbury on 14th April 1962. The triangular symbol in the nearside windscreen indicated a one-man operated vehicle. *(Geoff Coxon; D Akrigg Collection/J Copland)*

<< Opposite page: In 1952, for its batch of four AEC Regents, the 9613A version of the Mark III chassis was specified, fitted with crash gearbox. The lowbridge 55-seat bodywork was by Willowbrook. The crash gearboxes were later replaced by synchromesh units. Number **267** (**CJX 68**) is seen parked in Leeds ready to travel to Halifax on route 28. All four were withdrawn in 1964. Although Hebble at that time did not try to match fleet and registration numbers, it is a pity that these failed to coincide by one. *(Geoff Coxon)*

<< *Opposite page:* Four Leyland Royal Tiger PSU1/16 coaches fitted with Bellhouse Hartwell 37-seat Landmaster coach bodies, originally ordered by Blue Cars Ltd, of London, were delivered in 1954, registered ECP 205/6, 499 and 500, with fleet numbers 71-4. All four were withdrawn in 1966 and the chassis of this one was exported to Australia. The first of them numerically, No. **71** (**ECP 205**), is seen at Scarborough working on hire to Yelloway. This was not unusual: Hebble and Yelloway regularly hired vehicles from each other during the various Lancashire and West Riding "Wakes" weeks holiday periods. *(John Banks Collection/G H F Atkins)*

Above: The Bellhouse Hartwell coaches were renumbered 33-6 in 1957; the same vehicle is seen as No. **33** at the Gibbet Street end of the Halifax garage in front of the chassis-cleaning ramp. *(D Akrigg Collection)*

Below: Number **35** (**ECP 499**) at Westwood bus and coach station, Scarborough, in 1964. *(Geoff Coxon)*

Above: Numbers 75/6 (GCP 4/5), AEC Regent Mark V D3RV models with Weymann 55-seat bodywork, were the last lowbridge double-deckers delivered to and operated by Hebble. **GCP 5** is seen turning into Wellington Street, Leeds, from King Street with a good load of passengers. Although the route 15 destination shown is Burnley, the bus would travel only to Halifax; passengers for destinations beyond Halifax would transfer there to a single-decker. *(D Akrigg Collection/R F Mack)*

Below: Numbers 77-80 (GCP 6-9), delivered in 1956, were AEC Reliance MU3RV models with Willowbrook 44-seat bodies. These were the last buses to be delivered in coach livery. Number **80** (**GCP 9**) is seen in King Street, Leeds. *(Geoff Coxon)*

BH 53/6

BRADFORD—BINGLEY via WILSDEN.

Service 19

SUNDAYS.

				a.m.	a.m.	a.m.	p.m.		p.m.	p.m.	p.m.		p.m.
BRADFORD (Chester Street)	....	....	dep.	9 10	1030	1150	1230	then	5 50	6 20	6 50	then	9 50
Sandy Lane	....	....	,,	9 27	1047	1207	1247	every	6 07	6 37	7 07	every	1007
Wilsden (New Inn)	....	....	,,	9 35	1055	1215	1255	20 mins.	6 15	6 45	7 15	20 mins.	1015
Harden	....	....	,,	9 40	1100	1220	1 00	until	6 20	6 50	7 20	until	1020
BINGLEY (Central Area)	....	....	arr	9 48	1108	1228	1 08		6 28	6 58	7 28		1028

				a.m.	a.m.	p.m.	p.m.		p.m.	p.m.	p.m.		p.m.
BINGLEY (Central Area)	....	....	dep.	9 50	1110	1230	1 10	then	6 10	6 35	7 05	then	1030
Harden	....	....	,,	9 58	1118	1238	1 18	every	6 18	6 43	7 13	every	1038
Wilsden (Bank)	....	....	,,	1005	1125	1245	1 25	20 mins.	6 25	6 50	7 20	20 mins.	1045
Sandy Lane	....	....	,,	1011	1131	1251	1 31	until	6 31	6 56	7 26	until	1051
BRADFORD (Chester Street)	....	....	arr.	1028	1148	1 08	1 48		6 48	7 13	7 43		1108

BH 53/55

BRADFORD—BUTTERSHAW ESTATE.

Service 25

				WEEKDAYS			SUNDAYS		
				a.m.		p.m.	a.m.		p.m.
BRADFORD (Chester Street)	....	....	dep.	6 00	then	1030	1000	then	1030
Wibsey (Beacon Road)	....	....	,,	6 08	every	1038	1008	every	1038
BUTTERSHAW ESTATE (Junction Boltby Lane and Reevy Crescent)	....	arr.		6 12	30 mins. until	1042	1012	hour until	1042

				a.m.	then	p.m.	a.m.	then	p.m.
BUTTERSHAW ESTATE (Junction Boltby Lane and Reevy Crescent)	....	dep.		6 15	then	1045	1015	then	1045
Wibsey (Beacon Road)	....	....	,,	6 19	every	1049	1019	every	1049
BRADFORD (Chester Street)	....	....	arr.	6 27	30 mins. until	1057	1027	hour until	1057

From the timetable for 1st June 1955. *(Keith Healey Collection)*

BH 53/12
BH 53/41

HIPPERHOLME—LUMBROOK—SHELF—BRADFORD.
HIPPERHOLME—COLEY—SHELF—BRADFORD.

Services 26, 26a

DAILY SERVICE.

			NSu	NSu	NSu	NSu	NSu	NSu	NSu	NSu	NSu	NSu	NSu	NSu	NSu				
			a.m.	a.m.	a.m.	a.m.	a.m.	a.m.	a.m.	a.m.	a.m.	a.m.	a.m.	a.m.	p.m.	p.m.	p.m.	p.m.	p.m.
HIPPERHOLME (Denholme G. Rd.)	dep.		6 15	6 45	7 15	7 45	8 15	8 45	9 15	9 45	1015	1045	1115	1145	1215	1245	1 15	1 45	2 15
Coley Church	,,						8 20		9 20		1020		1120		1220		1 20		2 20
Lumbrook	,,		6 20	6 50	7 20	7 50		8 50		9 50		1050		1150		1250		1 50	
Shelf, Bottomley's Arms	,,		6 25	6 55	7 25	7 55	8 25	8 55	9 25	9 55	1025	1055	1125	1155	1225	1255	1 25	1 55	2 25
Wibsey	,,		6 31	7 01	7 31	8 01	8 31	9 01	9 31	1001	1031	1101	1131	1201	1231	1 01	1 31	2 01	2 31
BRADFORD (Chester Street)	arr		6 40	7 10	7 40	8 10	8 40	9 10	9 40	1010	1040	1110	1140	1210	1240	1 10	1 40	2 10	2 40

			Su	NSu														
			p.m.	p.m.	p.m.	p.m.	p.m.	p.m.	p.m.	p.m.	p.m.	p.m.	p.m.	p.m.	p.m.	p.m.	p.m.	p.m.
HIPPERHOLME (Denholme G. Rd.)	dep.		2 45	3 15	3 45	4 15	4 45	5 15	5 45	6 15	6 45	7 15	7 45	8 15	8 45	9 15	9 45	1015	1045
Coley Church	,,			3 20		4 20		5 20		6 20		7 20		8 20		9 20		1020	
Lumbrook	,,		2 50		3 50		4 50		5 20 5 50		6 50		7 50		8 50		9 50		1050
Shelf, (Bottomley's Arms)	,,		2 55	3 25	3 55	4 25	4 55	5 25	5 25 5 55	6 25	6 55	7 25	7 55	8 25	8 55	9 25	9 55	1025	1055
Wibsey	,,		3 01	3 31	4 01	4 31	5 01	5 31	5 31 6 01	6 31	7 01	7 31	8 01	8 31	9 01	9 31	1001	1031	1101
BRADFORD (Chester Street)	arr.		3 10	3 40	4 10	4 40	5 10	5 40	5 40 6 10	6 40	7 10	7 40	8 10	8 40	9 10	9 40	1010	1040	1110

			NSu	NSu	NSu	NSu	NSu	NSu	NSu	NSu	NSu	NSu	NSu	NSu		NSu		
			a.m.	a.m.	a.m.	a.m.	a.m.	a.m.	a.m.	a.m.	a.m.	a.m.	a.m.	a.m.	p.m.	p.m.	p.m.	p.m.
BRADFORD (Chester Street)	dep.		6 15	6 45	7 15	7 45	8 15	8 45	9 15	9 45	1015	1045	1115	1145	1215	1245	1 15	1 45 2 15
Wibsey	,,		6 23	6 53	7 23	7 53	8 23	8 53	9 23	9 53	1023	1053	1123	1153	1223	1253	1 23	1 53 2 23
Shelf (Bottomley's Arms)	,,		6 30	7 00	7 30	8 00	8 30	9 00	9 30	1000	1030	1100	1130	1200	1230	1 00	1 30	2 00 2 30
Lumbrook	,,		6 35	7 05	7 35	8 05	8 35		9 35		1035		1135	1205	1235		1 35		2 35
Coley Church	,,							9 05		1005		1105				1 05		2 05
HIPPERHOLME (Denholme G. Rd.)	arr.		6 40	7 10	7 40	8 10	8 40	9 10	9 40	1010	1040	1110	1140	1210	1240	1 10	1 40	2 10 2 40

			p.m.	p.m.	p.m.	p.m.	p.m.	p.m.	p.m.	p.m.	p.m.	p.m.	p.m.	p.m.	p.m.	p.m.	p.m.	p.m.
BRADFORD (Chester Street)	dep.		2 45	3 15	3 45	4 15	4 45	5 15	5 45	6 15	6 45	7 15	7 45	8 15	8 45	9 15	9 45	1015	1045
Wibsey	,,		2 53	3 23	3 53	4 23	4 53	5 23	5 53	6 23	6 53	7 23	7 53	8 23	8 53	9 23	9 53	1023	1053
Shelf (Bottomley's Arms)	,,		3 00	3 30	4 00	4 30	5 00	5 30	6 00	6 30	7 00	7 30	8 00	8 30	9 00	9 30	1000	1030	1100
Lumbrook	,,			3 35		4 35		5 35		6 35		7 35		8 35		9 35		1035	
Coley Church	,,		3 05		4 05		5 05		6 05		7 05		8 05		9 05		1005		1105
HIPPERHOLME (Denholme G. Rd.)	arr.		3 10	3 40	4 10	4 40	5 10	5 40	6 10	6 40	7 10	7 40	8 10	8 40	9 10	9 40	1010	1040	1110

NSu—Not on Sundays.   **Su**—Sundays Only.

Above: Having eliminated the Guy chassis from its fleet in 1952, Hebble borrowed three Arab double-deckers from City of Oxford Motor Services between December 1956 and April 1957. The vehicle illustrated, **JWL 910**, was a 1944 Arab II with Gardner 6LW engine and a 55-seat Roe utility body. The photograph was taken in Leeds. The Oxford Guys operated from the Company's Bradford depot. None of Hebble's services terminated at Odsal and it is likely that the vehicle was duplicating on the Halifax service carrying rugby league fans. The vehicle behind is an ex-London Transport utility Daimler in the fleet of the Executors of Samuel Ledgard. *(D Akrigg Collection/R F Mack)*

Below: Numbers 81-3 (GJX 845-7) were the first new highbridge double-deckers owned by Hebble. They were AEC Regent V D3RV models with Weymann 61-seat bodies, delivered in March 1957. Number **81** (**GJX 845**)

is seen descending Great Albion Street in Halifax, having just left the bus station, which is out of the picture to the left, bound for Bradford. The photograph was taken from the rooftop car park of the bowling alley. The bus was withdrawn in 1970. When these buses were delivered the fleet strength was 83, numbered 1-83. The management then made a decision to renumber the fleet. All single-deck buses had their fleet numbers increased by 100, all double-deckers by 200, and the three highbridge vehicles became 301-3. At this time Hebble acquired Ripponden and District Motors Ltd together with eleven coaches, and the coach fleet was renumbered in age order between 11 and 42. *(D Akrigg Collection/R F Mack)*

H EBBLE

MOTOR SERVICES LIMITED

PRIVATE HIRE

Whatever your travel requirements,

—————— consult us ——————

The benefit of our experience is at your disposal without obligation.

Write, call or 'phone
WALNUT STREET, HALIFAX
Tel. 2286

Above: The first of three 1951 ex-Ripponden and District ACB-bodied Leyland Royal Tiger PSU1/15 centre-entrance 41-seaters, No. **22** (**KWU 767**). All three were sold in 1960.

Below: Number **31** (**LWT 147**) was the first of a pair of Whitson-bodied AEC Regal IV 9621E models, which were also centre-entrance 41-seaters. They had been new to Ripponden and District in 1952 and were retained by Hebble until sale in 1960. LWT 147 saw further public service with Norfolk's, of Nayland. *(Both: D Akrigg Collection/R F Mack)*

HEBBLE ≡ RIBBLE

THROUGH FACILITIES AND CONNECTING SERVICES

HALIFAX — SOUTHPORT

HEBBLE SERVICE 15 BETWEEN HALIFAX AND BURNLEY AND RIBBLE EXPRESS SERVICE X5 BETWEEN BURNLEY AND SOUTHPORT.

TIME TABLE : 25th JUNE until 25th SEPTEMBER, 1955.

| TABLE 25 | HALIFAX, HEBDEN BRIDGE, BURNLEY, PRESTON, TARLETON and SOUTHPORT. | TABLE 25 |

Heavy Type times denote through coaches.

	Mons. to Fris. a.m.	Sats. only a.m.		Sats. only noon	Mons. to Fris. p.m.
Halifax, Bus Station ....dep.	7 30	**8 10**	**Southport,** Ribble Bus Station ......dep.	**12 0**	7 0
Hebden Bridge .... ,,	7 55	**8 35**	**Southport,** Jct. Albert & Park Roads ,,	**12 4**	7 4
Burnley, Cattle Market ....arr.	8 50	**9 29**	**Southport,** Jct. Cambridge & Marshside		
Burnley, Cattle Market ....dep.	**9 30**	**9 30**	Roads .... ,,	**12 7**	7 7
Preston, Ribble Bus Station ......arr.	1033	1033	**Tarleton,** A.A. Box .... ,,	1226	7 26
Tarleton, A.A. Box .... ,,	1059	1059	**Preston,** Ribble Bus Station ...... ,,	1252	7 52
Southport, Jct. Cambridge & Marshside ,,	1118	1118	**Burnley,** Cattle Market ....arr.	**1 54**	8 54
Roads.			**Burnley,** Cattle Market ....dep.	**1 55**	8 55
Southport, Jct. Albert & Park Roads ,,	1121	1121	**Hebden Bridge** ....arr.	**2 50**	9 50
Southport, Ribble Bus Station ......arr.	1125	1125	**Halifax,** Bus Station .... ,,	**3 15**	1015

PRINCIPAL FARES.

BETWEEN / AND	HALIFAX				HEBDEN BRIDGE			
	Adult		Child		Adult		Child	
	S	PR	S	PR	S	PR	S	PR
BURNLEY.............	2/2	3/4	1/1	1/8	1/7	2/3	10d.	1/2
PRESTON	4/8	7/1	2/4	3/8	4/1	6/–	2/1	3/2
SOUTHPORT	6/8	10/7	3/4	5/5	6/1	9/6	3/1	4/11

" S "—Single Fares.   " PR "—Period Return Fares.

BOOKING AND ENQUIRY OFFICES:

HEBBLE MOTOR SERVICES LTD.   Phone

| HALIFAX | .. | .. | .. | Fountain Street | .. | .. | .. | .. | .. | .. | 2624 |
| HEAD OFFICE | .. | .. | Walnut Street, Halifax | .. | .. | .. | .. | .. | 2286 |

RIBBLE MOTOR SERVICES LTD.   Phone

BURNLEY	..	..	..	Parker Lane	..	..	..	..	..	..	2171
PRESTON	..	..	30 Lancaster Road	..	..	..	..	..	4272
SOUTHPORT	..	..	Bus & Coach Station	..	..	..	..	..	55114
HEAD OFFICE	..	..	Frenchwood, Preston	..	..	..	..	..	4272

ADVANCE BOOKINGS MAY BE MADE ON THESE SERVICES.

The Services detailed herein are operated subject to the General Passenger Regulations and Conditions of the respective operators as set out in their published time tables and available for reference at their various offices.

mb. 3M. 10/12/54

Above: The remaining six ex-Ripponden coaches were Commers, of which Hebble No. **37** (**NWU 660**) is seen in Scarborough. An Avenger II, it had Plaxton 39-seat coachwork, had been new in 1954 and was sold by Hebble in 1962. It then served a further three owners, the last (Highland Omnibuses of Inverness) withdrawing it in 1967. *(Geoff Coxon)*

Below: In 1958 Hebble acquired Walton and Helliwell Ltd, of Mytholmroyd, from the Holdsworth group (the original owners of Hebble). The transaction included a further eleven vehicles, of which only six - all petrol-engined - were operated by Hebble. Bedford SB **SYG 561**, a 1957 Bedford SBG with Duple 41-seat coachwork, was the newest. It became Hebble No. **21** and is seen at Savile Park, Halifax. Sold in 1965, the coach worked for several subsequent owners and has survived into preservation. *(Hebble Collection)*

HEBBLE MOTOR SERVICES LTD.

AND

YELLOWAY MOTOR SERVICES LTD.

CONNECTING SERVICES AND THROUGH BOOKINGS TO

CHELTENHAM, GLOUCESTER BRISTOL, TAUNTON, EXETER, Etc.

TORQUAY

SUMMER SERVICE

DAILY

1st MAY, 1956 until 31st OCTOBER, 1956

READ DOWN Departure and Arrival Times SOUTHWARDS		Towns Served	Arrival and Departure Points	READ UP Departure and Arrival Times NORTHWARDS		Fares to and from Rochdale	
a.m.	F.S. p.m.			p.m.	F.S. p.m.	S.	P.R.
—	Dep. 6 15	Bradford	Chester Street Bus Station ...	—	Arr. 12 20	2/7	4/6
—	,, 6 30	Shelf	Bottomley's Arms	—	,, 12 03	2/-	3/6
Dep. 5 38 N.S.	,, 6 45	Halifax	Crossfield's Bus Station ...	Arr. 11 41	,, 11 41	1/8	2/8
,, 5 48 N.S.	,, 6 55	Sowerby Bridge	Station Road	,, 11 31	,, 11 31	1/5	2/5
,, 5 56 N.S.	Arr. 7 03	Ripponden	Bank	,, 11 22	,, 11 22	1/2	2/-
Arr. 6 34 N.S.	Arr. 7 41	Rochdale	*Smith Street...	Dep. 10 45	Dep. 10 45	S.	P.R.
Dep. 7 15	Dep. 7 45	Rochdale	Yelloway Coach Station, Weir St.	Arr. 10 45	Arr. 10 20	S.	P.R.
Arr. 11 05	Arr. 11 35	Wolverhampton	North Street, Opp. The Market	Dep. 6 55	Dep. 6 45	10/6	16/3
,, 11 45	,, 12 15	Kidderminster ...	Land Oak Hotel	,, 6 15	,, 6 05	16/6	22/6
,, 12 25	,, 12 55	Worcester	Express Bus Station	,, 5 35	,, 5 30	17/-	23/6
,, 1 25	,, 1 55	Cheltenham ...	Black & White Coach Station ...	,, 4 30	,, 4 30	21/-	27/6
Dep. 2 00	Dep. 2 25	Cheltenham ...	Black & White Coach Station ...	Arr. 4 00	Arr. 4 00	21/-	27/6
Arr. 2 24	Arr. 2 49	Gloucester... ...	India Road Coach Station ...	Dep. 3 36	Dep. 3 36	21/-	27/6
,, 3 56	,, 4 21	Bristol	Anchor Road	,, 2 04	,, 2 08	24/-	32/6
		Bristol	Anchor Road	Arr. 1 29			
,, 5 33	,, 5 48	Bridgwater ...	St. Mary's Street...	Dep. 12 02	,, 12 48	25/6	40/-
,, 6 00	,, 6 15	Taunton	Billett Street	,, 11 35	,, 12 20	26/-	41/-
Dep. 6 30		Taunton	Billett Street	Arr. 11 30			
	,, 7 35	Exeter	Paul Street Coach Station ...	Dep. 10 10	Dep. 11 00	33/-	48/-
Arr. 7 50		Exeter	Paul Street Coach Station ...		Arr. 10 40		
,, 8 40	,, 8 25	Newton Abbott	Railway Station Approach ...	,, 9 20	Dep. 9 55	37/6	55/-
,, 9 00	,, 8 45	Torquay	Town Hall Coach Station ...	Dep. 9 00	Dep. 9 30	37/6	55/-
p.m.	a.m.			a.m.	p.m.		

Fares to R'dale on the Hebble Section of the Route

Fares from Rochdale on the Yelloway Section of the Route

Above: Nineteen-fifty-eight saw the arrival of the first 30ft-long double-deckers, which were also the first to have forward entrances and platform doors. Numbers 304/5 (JCP 672/3) were AEC Regent V LD3RA models fitted with Weymann 71-seat bodywork. Number **305** (**JCP 673**) is illustrated in Halifax bus station. The other one, No. 304, was involved in a major accident because of brake failure and was repaired by Weymann's, returning thence bearing the fleet number 306. The Company was prosecuted as a consequence of the accident. Both vehicles were sold in 1970 and scrapped. *(D Akrigg)*

Below: Photographed at Scarborough, No. **187** (**KCP 889**) represents a pair of 1959 Willowbrook-bodied 43-seat AEC Reliances, which were the first underfloor-engined buses to carry bus livery from new. *(John Banks Collection/G H F Atkins)*

Above: Nineteen-fifty-nine also saw the arrival of Nos 43/4 (KJX 751/2), Plaxton-bodied 41-seat AEC Reliance 2MU3RV coaches. Both were sold in 1971. The first, No. **43** (**KJX 751**), was at Wembley Stadium for a Harlem Globettrotters event. *(R H G Simpson)*

Below: The second of these attractive vehicles, No. **44** (**KJX 752**), was photographed in Blackpool. Upon sale in 1971, KJX 752 was sold to the dealer North, of Sherburn in Elmet. The decomposing remains were still there in 1993. *(Geoff Coxon)*

Above: Number **310** (**LJX 201**) was the last of a batch of four 71-seat Weymann-bodied AEC Regent V 2D3RAs, new in 1959. The white radiator surround was a warning to staff that the vehicle was too high to enter Halifax depot via the entrance nearest to Hopwood Lane. The practice was discontinued when the depot was rebuilt and a new bus washer installed. LJX 201 was sold in 1971. *(Senior Transport Archive)*

Below: Number **307** (**LJX 198**) of the same batch is seen, after repainting into normal livery, on the Halifax to Leeds service. It was sold in 1970 and in the late 1970s was bought for preservation and restored. It is currently stored in Halifax awaiting a second restoration. *(D Akrigg)*

Above: The impressive Cavalier body by Thomas Harrington, of Hove, entered the Hebble fleet in 1960 on three 41-seat AEC Reliance 2MU3RV chassis. Number **12** (**MCP 819**), the first of the trio, is seen in Bay E of Halifax bus station on 20th April 1968, ready to depart on an excursion to Morecambe. Note the condition of the road surface. The coach was sold in 1971, had three later owners and was scrapped in 1978. *(D Akrigg)*

Below: Number **312** (**NCP 474**) was the first of two 1960 AEC Regent V 2D3RAs with Metro-Cammell 71-seat bodywork. In 1971, when Hebble ceased to operate stage carriage services, this bus passed to the Halifax Joint Omnibus Committee (later Calderdale JOC), who sold it in 1972. After a succession of subsequent owners, a South Wales operator converted it as a recovery vehicle in the late 1970s. Out of use by 1980, it is presumed scrapped. *(Senior Transport Archive)*

Above: Number **192** (**NCP 382**) was a 1961 Park Royal-bodied AEC Reliance 2MU3RV model fitted out as a 43-seat service bus. It was photographed passing through Boothtown in the direction of Halifax. In 1971 it passed to Halifax JOC, and was withdrawn by the successor Calderdale in 1972. It ran in Lancashire briefly before being scrapped in 1974. *(D Akrigg Collection/ J Copland)*

Below: An interior view of one of Hebble's standard BET-style underfloor-engined single-deckers. *(Senior Transport Archive)*

Above: The first of a trio of Ford 570E Duple-bodied 41-seaters, No. **48** (**OCP 87**) was new in 1961. It was sold after suffering an accident in 1970 and was scrapped in 1974. *(Senior Transport Archive)*

Below: AEC Regent V No. **277** (**PCP 403**) crosses North Bridge on its way into Halifax from Bradford via Queensbury. A Northern Counties-bodied 65-seater new in 1962, it was sold in 1971 and scrapped in Carlisle in 1975. All the buildings visible in the picture have been demolished as part of road improvement schemes. *(D Akrigg)*

Above: Alexander bodywork was specified for three 1962 AEC Reliance 2MU3RA 43-seat service buses delivered in June of that year. The first of them was No. **194** (**PCP 802**), illustrated when brand new at Alexander's factory. Following accident damage, it was withdrawn in 1971. *(Senior Transport Archive)*

Below: The first 36ft-long service buses arrived in 1962 in the shape of Nos 100/1 (RCP 131/2), Willowbrook-bodied 53-seat AEC Reliance 2U3RA models. These were standard BET vehicles and No. **101** (**RCP 132**) was photographed in Halifax bus station on 30th May 1970. It was withdrawn the following year. *(D Akrigg)*

Above: The only AEC Regent V of type 2D3RA to carry a Northern Counties body was No. **314** (**RCP 237**), a 71-seater new in September 1962. From April to June 1968 it was loaned to Yorkshire Traction in exchange for some of their smaller vehicles because of a weight restriction on North Bridge, Halifax. It was sold to Yorkshire (WD) in December 1968 and bought back in 1969, passing to Halifax Corporation in 1971. It later ran for the Halifax JOC and for the West Yorkshire PTE. Finally withdrawn in 1976 it passed into preservation in 1981 and is believed to still exist.

Below: Numbers **71/2** (**RJX 871/2**) were Plaxton-bodied 47-seat Leyland PSU3/3R Leopards new in 1963 and withdrawn in 1973. They were the first 36ft-long coaches and were photographed in Halifax depot yard. *(Both: D Akrigg)*

Above: Numbers 102-5 (SCP 562-5) were 1963 Leyland PSU3/1R Leopards with 53-seat Willowbrook bodywork. All four were transferred to Yorkshire (WD) in 1971. The vehicle illustrated, No. **103** (**SCP 563**), was photographed in King Street, Leeds. *(Geoff Coxon)*

Below: In May 1964 Hebble took delivery of a Bedford VAS1 with Plaxton Embassy 29-seat coachwork. It was numbered **41** and registered **TCP 897**. Withdrawn in 1971, it saw further service with a variety of operators until 1979. *(Senior Transport Archive)*

Above: The lightweight theme continued in 1964 with the purchase of No. **53** (**TCP 898**), a Plaxton-bodied Ford 570E 41-seater, seen here at Scarborough with Oliver's Mount prominent in the background. Following withdrawal in 1971 it ran for a Nottinghamshire independent until 1976.

Below: In sharp contrast to the lightweight Bedford and Ford coaches, 1964 also produced four AEC Reliance 2U3RA models: two Alexander-bodied 49-seat coaches and two Marshall-bodied buses. One of the 49-seaters, No. **74** (**TCP 900**), was also photographed at Scarborough. In the background is **DBT 553**, an East Yorkshire ex-Everingham Brothers utility Daimler, in use as a left luggage office. Model collectors should check the recent EFE model of this bus, which has a Guy radiator. *(Both: Geoff Coxon)*

Above: Scarborough in 1964 produced this photograph of another of that year's new Hebble vehicles. The AEC Reliance chassis, in 2U3RA form, was used for a pair of 51-seat Marshall Camagna-bodied service buses. The second, No. **107** (**TCP 902**), is illustrated. It passed to Yorkshire (WD) in 1971 and was withdrawn in 1975, subsequently running for Black Prince Coaches and Irvine of Law before moving on to a contractor in 1977. *(Geoff Coxon)*

Below: The last AEC Regent Vs bought new by Hebble were 1964's Nos 315/6 (AJX 409/10B). They were the 2D3RA version, fitted with Weymann 72-seat bodywork. Number **316** (**AJX 410B**) was photographed at Boothtown, on the way from Bradford to Halifax via Queensbury. Both vehicles followed the familiar path into the Halifax JOC fleet, later Calderdale JOC and West Yorkshire PTE, and both were withdrawn in 1976 and sold for scrap. *(D Akrigg Collection/J Copland))*

Above: Nineteen-sixty-five's deliveries again saw a lightweight Ford joining the fleet as well as a number of heavyweights in the form of AEC Reliances. One of the latter, No. **131** (**BJX 131C**) photographed when brand new, is representative of a batch of four 2MU4RA models with dual-purpose 39-seat coachwork by Park Royal. The vehicle had a varied history after passing from Hebble to Yorkshire (WD) in 1971: it ran in turn for West Riding, a Welsh independent and finally a scout troop before being scrapped in 1983.

Below: Number **75** (**BJX 75C**), also new in 1965, was a 2U3RA-type AEC Reliance with Plaxton 47-seat coachwork. It was sold after only seven years of service and then worked for two independents until 1976. *(Both: Senior Transport Archive)*

The only rear-engined vehicle bought new by Hebble was No. **351** (**DJX 351D**) in 1966. A Daimler CRG6LX Fleetline, it had a Northern Counties 75-seat body and was new in July of that year. It was photographed when brand new in Halifax bus station *(above)* and in Broad Street, Halifax. In 1971 it passed to Yorkshire (WD), for whom it ran briefly before moving on to the Halifax Joint Omnibus Committee and its successors. In 1984 it was sold for preservation but in the event was exported to the United States of America and converted to open-top specification. *(Both: Trevor Hartley)*

Above: Interesting second-hand vehicles were three Leyland L1 Leopards with 41-coach-seat Burlingham bus bodies, acquired in 1970. They had been new to the Sheffield "C" fleet in 1960. After the familiar transfers to Halifax JOC and Calderdale all were withdrawn in 1972 and exported to the Irish Republic. Number **160** (**5875 W**), the first of the three, was photographed on the parking area near Halifax bus station on the X12 from Bradford to Manchester. For a short while Hebble worked this service jointly with the North Western Road Car Company after taking it over from Yorkshire (WD). *(Senior Transport Archive)*

Below: Other second-hand, and rather more uncommon, vehicles for Hebble were four 1963 AEC 4MU3RA Reliances with the very rare (only six were built) Duple Dragonfly 49-seat coach body, acquired from the Samuelson New Transport Company, of London, in 1968. Number **82** (**448 FXX**), here, also on the X12, displaying a paper destination sticker for Manchester, was converted as a car transporter after withdrawal in 1970 *(D Akrigg)*

Above: Numbers 417-22 (LJX 817-22H) were the last vehicles delivered in true Hebble livery, one of so many lost to the National Bus Company's insipid all-over white. Leyland PSU3A/4R Leopards, they had Plaxton Panorama Elite 47-seat coach bodies and were new in May 1970. The former No. 422 (**LJX 822H**), renumbered in 1971 as **57**, is seen soon after passing in 1974 to National Travel (North East). The vehicle operated for Crosville between 1979 and 1982. *(D Akrigg)*

Below: Although owned by National Travel (North East), to which Hebble had changed its name in January 1974, No. **69** (**YWE 497M**), a Duple-bodied Bedford YRT, was still carrying the Hebble fleetname when photographed in Blackpool. *(Geoff Coxon)*

HEBBLE IN COLOUR

Above: In the last few months of Hebble's stage carriage operations the tow truck became a familiar sight. Here it is seen at Shelf rescuing No. **604** (**DHD 186**), an ex-Yorkshire (WD) 1959 AEC Regent V that had been transferred to Hebble in May 1969. A 70-seater, the body was by Metro-Cammell. The bus went on to more exotic climes when it joined the fleet of the China Motor Bus Company, Hong Kong, in 1972. *(Nicholas Harris)*

Below: Hebble AEC Regents at Halifax bus station on different routes to Bradford. The Regent III, No. **269** (**CJX 70**), was scheduled to cover the distance three minutes faster than the Regent V, No. **276** (**GCP 5**); the 29 was known as "the Wibsey Flier". *(Nicholas Harris Collection/Vic Nutton)*

Above: Numbers **275/6** (**GCP 4/5**) pictured in the Halifax depot yard on 23rd June 1968 on the occasion of a visit by The Omnibus Society. When new these vehicles were described in an enthusiast magazine as "the ugliest buses in Yorkshire". They were both withdrawn in 1968 and went to North's. Neither ran again. *(Nicholas Harris)*

Below: Number **312** (**NCP 475**), a 1960 Metro-Cammell-bodied AEC Regent V, photographed in Lord Street, Huddersfield, prior to departing for Bradford on route 64. The route was jointly operated with Bradford and Huddersfield Corporations and for many years each operator had a different route number (Hebble called it the 12); even the fare stage numbers were different: pity the poor Inspector trying to check tickets on another operator's vehicle. Eventually they agreed to standardise. *(Both: Nicholas Harris Collection/Vic Nutton)*

Above: Number **617** (**PCP 405**) - formerly No. 279 - is seen at the bottom of Bay E in Halifax bus station on the Leeds service on 20th February 1971. A 1962 AEC Regent V, its Northern Counties front-entrance body had 65 seats. *(Nicholas Harris)*

Below: The next bus in the numbering system, No. **618** (**PCP 406**), had been No. 280 from 1962, when it was new, to 1970. It was photographed in Halifax bus station on 28th February 1971 awaiting its departure time for Bradford - for the last time. *(Peter Cain)*

Above: Number **284** (**DHD 184**) was another of the Metro-Cammell-bodied AEC Regent Vs transferred from Yorkshire (WD) to Hebble in September 1969. It was allocated the new fleet number 602 in 1970, but never carried it. In this 21st November 1970 picture it is turning into Halifax bus station from St James's Road, with an "On Hire to Hebble" sticker in the bulkhead window. The bus station was later demolished, although the setts, of historical importance, remain.

Below: Photographed in Halifax bus station on 1st March 1970, No. **350** (**BHD 222C**), a 1966 Alexander-bodied 75-seat Daimler CRG6LX Fleetline, was the only second-hand rear-engined bus bought by Hebble. It came from Yorkshire (WD) in 1969, to whom it returned in 1971 for five months before being bought by Halifax Corporation. It later passed to West Yorkshire PTE who sold it in 1978 for scrap. *(Both: Nicholas Harris)*

Above: Number **301** (**GJX 845**), the first Hebble highbridge double-decker, was sold to W North (PV) Ltd at Sherburn in Elmet in April 1970 and was photographed there on 16th May alongside a Wilts & Dorset Bristol KSW and a Rhondda AEC Regent. GJX 845 was sold on by North's in July 1970, probably for scrap.

Below: Number **165** (**CJX 66**), a 1953 Leyland PSU1/13 Royal Tiger with Weymann bodywork, was photographed in Halifax depot yard shortly before its 1966 withdrawal. The unattractive building to the rear of the vehicle housed the bus washer. *(Both: Nicholas Harris)*

Above: Number **178** (**GCP 7**) was a Willowbrook-bodied AEC Reliance 44-seater dating from May 1956. It is seen climbing out of Cullingworth up Manywells Brow on route 2 from Bingley to Halifax.

Below: The same bus was photographed in the rain at North's Sherburn in Elmet yard on 6th August 1968 alongside an ex-East Yorkshire Willowbrook-bodied Leyland Tiger Cub. GCP 7 looked to be in good condition but was nonetheless sold on for scrap in 1970. *(Both: Nicholas Harris)*

Above: Number **194** (**PCP 802**), one of the 1962 Alexander-bodied AEC Reliances, photographed in a gloomy Rochdale at the terminus of route 28.

Below: On 6th September 1969 No. **159** (**GHD 759**), a Marshall-bodied AEC Reliance recently acquired from Yorkshire (WD), was photographed in Halifax bus station. The vehicle was never repainted into Hebble's version of a red and white livery and was sold in 1971. *(Both: Nicholas Harris)*

Above: Another ex-Yorkshire (WD) vehicle to find its way into Hebble service was No. 186 (**DHD 201**), a 1959 Park Royal-bodied AEC Reliance 43-seater acquired in November 1968. Renumbered **650** in 1970, it was photographed at the Hipperholme terminus of route 26 to Bradford on 2nd January 1971, very soon before its withdrawal in the following month.

Below: Number **162** (**5877 W**), a 1960 Burlingham-bodied Leyland L1 Leopard, was photographed in Walnut Street, Halifax, on 19th July 1970, having recently been acquired from Sheffield. By 1980 it was a shed in Galway. *(Both: Nicholas Harris)*

Above: Another of the buses transferred from Yorkshire (WD) in 1969 was No. **659** (**FHD 126**), a 1960 AEC Reliance with Park Royal bodywork. Again, it retained YWD livery, as shown in this photograph taken on 20th February 1971 in Halifax bus station. It was withdrawn a few weeks later in March.

Below: One of the striking Bellhouse Hartwell-bodied Leyland Royal Tigers, No. **35** (**ECP 499**), in a mid-sixties "Wakes" Saturday view at Blackwall, Halifax. On such occasions thousands of holidaymakers left Halifax for the east and west coast resorts and anything that moved, together with many hired vehicles, would be pressed into service. *(Both: Nicholas Harris)*

Above: The driver of No. **10** (**KJX 751**), a 1959 Plaxton-bodied AEC Reliance, relaxes with his newspaper in Blackpool on 6th October 1968.

Below: Number **15** (**MCP 821**), a 1960 AEC Reliance with Harrington Cavalier coachwork, is posed for the photographer outside Hebble's Bradford depot in Park Lane on 30th March 1968. *(Both: Nicholas Harris)*

Above: Less common in the group fleets than they were in those of independents, the Duple-bodied Ford 570E invariably looked attractive in the company operators' liveries. Hebble's No. **48** (**OCP 87**) features in a view at Ambler Thorn, near Queensbury, on 23rd June 1968.

Below: It often happened that lightweight chassis, such as the Ford shown above and this 1967 Bedford VAS1, did not last long in the company fleets: cheaper to purchase than the Reliances and Leopards, they were no doubt deliberately written down over a shorter period. Number **42** (**FCP 842E**), with its Plaxton 25-seat coachwork, was sold in 1971 when only four years old. The Bradford depot photograph was taken on 23rd June 1968. *(Both: Nicholas Harris)*

Above: Supporting the "short life for lightweights" theory, Plaxton-bodied Ford 570E No. **53** (**TCP 898**) came in 1964 and went in 1971. The 41-seater was photographed on 19th July 1970 on the waste ground adjacent to Victoria Road, Halifax.

Below: Number **80** (**HJX 980F**) was firmly in the heavyweight category, yet lasted a mere seven years - proving an exception to the rule - in the Hebble and then Yorkshire (WD) fleets. A Willowbrook-bodied dual-purpose 49-seat AEC Reliance, it was new in June 1968, passed to YWD in 1971 and was withdrawn in 1975. It was subsequently owned by a health authority and a morris-dancing troupe. This is another 23rd June 1968 picture at Bradford depot. *(Both: Nicholas Harris)*

Above: Here is one of the 1970 Plaxton-bodied Leyland Leopards *(see page 80)* that were the last vehicles delivered in Hebble red and cream livery, still in those much-missed colours. Number **417** (**LJX 817H**) was at Chester Street, Bradford, on 2nd January 1971. On 1st January 1974 it passed to National Travel (North East) and to Crosville in 1979. It later ran for an independent, with whom the fitting of a second-hand body apparently necessitated a "Q" registration plate.

Below: Number **24** (**6309 WJ**) was a 1962 Plaxton-bodied AEC Reliance acquired from Sheffield United Tours in 1969. It was at Gibbet Street, Halifax, on 19th July 1970, and was sold in 1971. *(Both: Nicholas Harris)*

Above: A Hebble coach that ended its days in 1978 a long way from Yorkshire - with Garelochhead Coach Services, to whom it went after withdrawal in 1975 from the National Travel (North East) fleet. New in 1967 to Hebble, No. **29** (**FJX 171E**) was a Plaxton-bodied 41-seat AEC Reliance 6MU3R. The photograph was taken in Great Albion Street, close to Halifax bus station.

Below: In June 1970 the entire Yorkshire (WD) coach fleet passed into Hebble ownership together with the former's licences. One of the coaches was No. **22** (**KHD 905**), a 1964 Plaxton-bodied 49-seat Leyland Leopard, which was photographed in Cheltenham on 3rd April 1972 operating on the South-West Clipper with the Yelloway service coach to Bradford behind. KHD 905 was sold in 1974 and exported to Ireland. *(Both: Nicholas Harris)*

Above: We are fortunate to have colour images of what were perhaps Hebble's most exotic coaches (challenged, maybe, only by the Bellhouse Hartwell machines) - the Duple Continental- and Dragonfly-bodied machines. Number **81** (**280 HLC**) was of the former type, and was a 1964 AEC Reliance acquired in 1968 from Red Line Continental Motorways Ltd, of London. It was photographed on 23rd June 1968 at Ambler Thorn, near Queensbury and was withdrawn in 1971.

Below: The ultra-rare Duple Dragonfly *(see page 79)* is represented in colour by another view of No. **82** (**448 FXX**). It was photographed in Halifax depot yard. If any bus enthusiasts lived in the terraced houses alongside the yard, life must have seemed heaven on earth. *(Both: Nicholas Harris)*

Above: **LJX 817H** at Gallowgate, Newcastle upon Tyne. A 1970 Leyland Leopard, bodied by Plaxton, ordered by Yorkshire (WD) but delivered to Hebble as fleet number 417, it had just passed into the National Travel (East) fleet in 1977, having been owned by National Travel (North East) as No. 52 since 1st January 1974. After 1st February of that year the use of fleet numbers was discontinued and registration numbers alone used for identifying vehicles. *(Geoff Coxon)*

Below: Hebble in preservation: No. **307** (**LJX 198**) is seen at Sandtoft soon after restoration *(see page 68). (John Senior)*